編者的話

在今天這個國際化的社會，不只是外商公司，就連本國企業也多與外國公司有業務往來，必須經常接待外國訪客。身為上司左右手的秘書，一口流利的英語就成為必備的條件。「**秘書英語自學手冊**」（ *A Mini-Handbook for Secretaries* ）就是要提供專業秘書們一個輕鬆自學英會話的方法。本書根據秘書工作所需，模擬實況場景，設計自學內容，即使是社會新鮮人，亦能在短期內入行。

全書採一單元一場景的編排方式，涵括秘書與上司、公司同事和外國客戶間的各式接觸。每個單元包括**實況對話**（ *sample dialogue* ）與**代換語句**（ *substitution drills* ），使您經由反覆練習，熟悉各種句型，靈活運用。單元後有基本對話測驗，可加深印象，讓您在不同場合中，養成英語脫口而出的習慣。

除了流利的英語外，優秀秘書還必須精通實務技巧。「**秘書小點子**」（ *a tip for you* ）告訴您接打電話、招待訪客、安排業務旅行、處理檔案等必備小常識，並介紹**最新OA設備**，如 *fax, word processor* 等，面面俱到，幫助您掌握時代訊息，提高工作效率。

審慎的編校過程，是我們堅持的原則，若仍有疏漏之處，還望各界先進不吝指正。

Editorial Staff

● 企劃 / 陳瑠琍

● 英文撰稿

　Edward C. Yulo・Christiaan Virant

　Vincent Bertino・Thomas Deneau

　Jean Li

● 校訂

　劉　毅・陳怡平・林佩汀・王慶銘

　劉瑞芬・鄭明俊・林順隆

● 翻譯 / 許文美

● 封面設計 / 白雪嬌

● 版面設計 / 陳燕玉・張鳳儀

● 版面構成 / 蘇淑玲

● 插畫 / 白雪嬌・黃美倫

● 打字 / 黃淑貞・倪秀梅・吳秋香

CHAPTER 1

Dialogues with the Boss

與上司溝通

CHAPTER 2　Communications with Various Publics
與外界交際

CHAPTER 3

Interoffice Communications

與同事聯繫

CHAPTER 4

Telephone Calls

以電話應對

CHAPTER 1

Dialogues with the Boss

與上司溝通

UNIT 1

A Morning Report
工作報告

SAMPLE DIALOGUE／實況對話

Mr. Baker : What's my schedule for today, Sandra?
珊德拉，告訴我今天的日程表。

Sandra : Yes, you are supposed to meet the president
at ten fifteen this morning. Then, you have
a lunch appointment with Mr. Clark. And
this afternoon at three you are scheduled to
speak before a group of seminar participants.
好的，你今天早上十點十五分要見總經理。然後，午餐
時和克拉克先生有約。下午三點鐘要在討論會上演講。

Mr. Baker : Do you have the Financial Report ready?
那份財務報告妳準備好了嗎？

Sandra : Certainly. 當然。

** schedule〔ˊskɛdʒʊl〕n. 時間表 v. 排定 *seminar participant* 參與討論會者

SUBSTITUTION DRILLS／代換語句 ▨▨▨▨▨▨▨▨▨▨▨▨▨▨▨▨▨▨▨

1.

You	are supposed are scheduled are	to meet the president at ten.

➡ 十點鐘你必須去見總經理。

2.

You have a	lunch appointment working lunch dinner meeting	with Mr. Li.

➡ 午餐／晚餐時你要會見李先生。

3.

Would you like me to brief you on	your schedule for today? what's scheduled for today?

➡ 你要不要我對你今天的時間安排，做個簡短的報告？

4.

The Financial Report	is ready. won't be ready till next week. is being edited right now.

➡ 那份財務報告準備好了／下禮拜才能準備好／現在正在修改。

** brief〔brif〕v. 對～做簡短說明　　edit〔ˈɛdɪt〕v. 修改

5.

Do you have any	special particular specific	instruction for this ?

➡ 對於這個，你有沒有任何特別的指示？

** specific〔spɪˈsɪfɪk〕*adj*. 特別的

EXERCISE /練習

◉ 模仿前面範例，完成下列對話。

　　Boss : What's _____ for today, _____ ?

Secretary : Yes, you _____ to meet Mr. Blake at ten

　　　　　　fifteen this morning. Then, you have a _____

　　　　　　with Ms. Crane. At one o'clock, you are

　　　　　　scheduled to speak before _____ .

　　Boss : Is the Financial Report ready?

Secretary : _____ .

KEY TO EXERCISE /解答

1. my schedule, Jill, are scheduled, lunch appointment, the board, Certainly

2. on the appointment book, Rachel, are, meeting, a convention, Yes

UNIT 2　Typing/Word Processing
打字／文書處理

Is this a rough draft?

SAMPLE DIALOGUE／實況對話

Mr. Baker : Sandra, could you please type this report for me? 珊德拉，請替我打這份報告好嗎？

Sandra : Certainly, Mr. Baker. Is this a rough draft? 當然，貝克先生。這是初稿嗎？

Mr. Baker : Yes it is. Could you please double space it so I can make corrections? 是的。妳能不能隔行打？這樣我才好刪改。

Sandra : Yes, I will. Do you need it finished right away? 好的。你現在就要嗎？

Mr. Baker : No. Sometime this afternoon will be fine. 不，今天下午完成就可以了。

** rough〔rʌf〕 *adj.* 未修飾的　　draft〔dræft〕 *n.* 草稿

SUBSTITUTION DRILLS／代換語句

1.

Certainly, Of course, Right away,	Mr. Baker. Is this a	rough final	draft?

➡ 當然／馬上好，貝克先生。這是初／完稿嗎？

2.

Do you need it	finished completed typed	right away?

➡ 你要我馬上完成／打好嗎？

3.

Which mailing list should I	key type put	this in?

➡ 我應該把這份存入哪一個郵件檔案中？

4.

Should I	double space? single space? triple space?

➡ 我應該隔行打／不隔行打／打一行空二行嗎？

** triple〔'trɪpl̟〕v. 使成三倍

5.

Which	font letter type letterhead	should I use?

➡ 我應該用什麼字體／信紙呢？

** font 〔fɑnt〕 *n.* 一套字體
letterhead 〔'lɛtɚ,hɛd〕 *n.* 印有信頭文字的信紙

EXERCISE／練習

◉ 模仿前面範例，完成下列對話。

Boss : _____ , could you please type this
_____ for me?

Secretary : _____ , Mr. Thompson. Is it a rough
draft?

Boss : _____ . Could you please double space
it so I can make _____ ?

Secretary : Yes, I will. Do you _____ it finished
right away?

Boss : No. _____ will be fine.

KEY TO EXERCISE / 解答

1. Miss Lee, report, Certainly, Yes it is, corrections, need, Sometime this afternoon

2. Stella, letter, Immediately, No it isn't, some changes, have to have, Anytime today

---

A TIP FOR YOU / 秘書小點子

打字是秘書必備的基本技能，然而修改、增減內容或更動內容順序等，常使得打字變成不斷重覆而令人厭煩的工作。隨著**文書處理機**（ *word processor* ）的廣泛應用，打字不再是件苦差事。它和電腦一樣，只要按幾個鍵，就可以任意修改、增減、調動順序、組合文件，而不必整篇重打；而且利用**印表機**（ *printer* ），可以複製無數份原稿（ original ）， 這對於製作信文內容相同而收信人不同的**同文信函**（ *form letter* ）尤其方便。此外，使用文書處理機來儲存檔案，不論歸檔、調檔都十分容易。文書處理機可提高秘書的工作效率，從而改善工作品質，是現代秘書的好幫手。

UNIT 3　Filing
歸檔

SAMPLE DIALOGUE / 實況對話

Mr. Baker : Please file all these reports for me.
　　　　　　請替我把這些報告歸檔。

Sandra : Do you want me to file them in alphabetical order? 你要我依字母順序歸檔嗎？

Mr. Baker : No, please file them according to dates.
　　　　　　不，請依照日期順序。

Sandra : I'll make copies and file them both ways.
　　　　　　我會影印一份，然後兩種方式各歸檔一份。

Mr. Baker : Great idea! You are an excellent secretary.
　　　　　　好主意！妳真是個好秘書。

Sandra : Of course I am, sir. 當然囉，先生。

＊＊ file〔faɪl〕v.歸檔　alphabetical〔͵ælfə`bɛtɪkḷ〕adj.按字母順序的

SUBSTITUTION DRILLS／代換語句

1.

Do you want me to Would you like me to Should I	file them	in alphabetical order? alphabetically? according to dates?

➡ 你要我依字母／日期順序歸檔嗎？

2.

I'll	make copies copy them duplicate them	and file them both ways.

➡ 我會影印一份，然後兩種方式各歸檔一份。

3.

I'll	list down organize photocopy	all the documents on this file.

➡ 我會將檔案內所有文件編目／整理／影印好。

4.

Should I	file all these reports put these reports in the files file these documents	now?

➡ 我現在必須將這些報告／文件全部歸檔嗎？

＊＊ duplicate〔'djuplə,ket〕v. 複印　photocopy〔'fotə,kɑpɪ〕v. 影印
document〔'dɑkjəmənt〕n. 文件

5.

Which	file folder	do you want me to file this in?

➡ 你要我把這一件存入哪一個檔案／檔案夾裏？

＊＊ folder〔'foldə〕 *n.* 檔案夾

EXERCISE／練習

◉ 模仿前面範例，完成下列對話。

   Boss : Please file these _____ for me.
Secretary : _____ me to file them _____ ?

   Boss : No, please file them according to dates.
Secretary : I'll _____ and file them both ways.

   Boss : _____ idea! You are _____ secretary.
Secretary : Of course I am, sir.

KEY TO EXERCISE／解答

1. reports, Do you want, in alphabetical order, make copies,
   Great, an excellent

2. documents, Would you like, alphabetically, copy them, Good,
   a wonderful

UNIT 4 Writing Letters
寫信

SAMPLE DIALOGUE／實況對話

Mr. Baker : Sandra, could you come in for a moment?
珊德拉，請進來一下好嗎？

Sandra : Sure. Let me just turn off the typewriter.
好。我先把打字機關掉。

Mr. Baker : Send a letter to Mr. Owen asking him about the delays in his monthly installments. If there's no reply within a week, write him a demand letter.
寫一封信給歐文先生，問他有關分期付款未繳的事。如果一星期之內沒有答覆，就寫信催款。

Sandra : Alright. I'll have it typed up right away.
好，我會馬上打好。

** delay 〔dɪˈle〕 n. 延遲　installment 〔ɪnˈstɔlmənt〕 n. 分期付款

SUBSTITUTION DRILLS / 代換語句

1.

Let me just	turn off shut off switch off	the typewriter.

➡ 我先把打字機關掉。

2.

I'll have it	typed up printed	right away.

➡ 我會馬上打好／印好。

3.

Let me	just repeat this again. repeat what you've said. see if I got this right.

➡ 讓我重覆一遍／重覆你剛才說的／看看我聽的對不對。

4.

Do we need to enclose	his receipts? the terms of the contract? his payment schedule?

➡ 我們需要附寄他的收據／契約書／付款時間表嗎？

** enclose〔ɪnˈkloz〕v. 附寄 　　 receipt〔rɪˈsit〕n. 收據
　　terms〔tɝmz〕n. pl. 條件 　　 contract〔ˈkɑntrækt〕n. 契約

5.

| Whom shall I | address
send
write | this letter to ? |

➡ 我應該將這封信寄給誰呢 ？

6.

| Do you want
me to | use the typewriter or the computer?
bring out his file ?
check his accounts ? |

➡ 你要我用打字機還是電腦／找出他的檔案嗎／查他的存款嗎 ？

** account 〔 ə'kaʊnt 〕 *n.* 存款帳戶

EXERCISE / 練習

● 模仿前面範例 , 完成下列對話 。

Boss : Emily, could you _____ ?

Secretary : Sure. Let me just _____ the typewriter.

Boss : _____ a letter to Mr. Hardy _____ him about _____ . If there's no _____ within a week, write him _____ .

Secretary : Alright. I'll _____ right away.

KEY TO EXERCISE／解答

1.　come into my office, turn off, Send, asking, back installments, reply, a demand letter, do it

2.　spare a minute, switch off, Write, warning, his overdue accounts with us, answer, again, type it

═ 國 際 函 件 資 費 表 ═

函 件 種 類	航空函件資費（水陸及航空混合）				
	計 費 標 準	香 港澳 門	亞 洲大洋洲	歐非中南美洲各地	美 國加拿大
信　　　　函（每件限重不逾二公斤）	不逾 20 公克	9.00			
	每續重 20 公克	6.00			
	不逾 10 公克		13.00	17.00	15.00
	每續重 10 公克		9.00	14.00	13.00
印　刷　物（每件限重不逾二公斤書籍得展至五公斤）	不逾 20 公克	7.00	10.00	13.00	13.00
	每續重 20 公克	5.00	7.00	10.00	10.00

資 費 類 別	計　費　標　準	資　費
掛 號 費	除水陸資費或航空資費外每件另加	24.00
快 遞 費	除水陸資費或航空資費外每件另加	30.00

國內函件資費表

(一)普通資費

類　　　　　　別	計　費　標　準	資　費 (新台幣元)
信　　　　　函 （每件限重不逾二公斤）	不逾 20 公克	5.00
	逾 20 公克不逾 50 公克	10.00
	逾 50 公克不逾 100 公克	15.00
	逾 100 公克不逾 250 公克	25.00
	逾 250 公克不逾 500 公克	45.00
	逾 500 公克不逾 1 公斤	80.00
	逾 1 公斤不逾 2 公斤	130.00
印　　刷　　物 （每件限重不逾二公斤 單本書籍得展至五公斤）	不逾 50 公克	3.50
	逾 50 公克不逾 100 公克	7.50
	逾 100 公克不逾 250 公克	10.00
	逾 250 公克不逾 500 公克	20.00
	逾 500 公克不逾 1 公斤	35.00
	逾 1 公斤不逾 2 公斤	55.00
	每續重 1 公斤	20.00

(二)特種資費

資　　費　　別	計　費　標　準		資　費 (新台幣元)
航　　空　　費	除普通資費外，每重 20 公克另加		2.00
掛　　號　　費	除資 普費 通外加	每件	14.00
限　時　專　送　費		每件	7.00

UNIT 5 Making Copies
影印

SAMPLE DIALOGUE / 實況對話

Mr. Baker : Could you copy this report for me?
    妳能幫我影印這份報告嗎？

Sandra : Certainly. How many copies would you like?
    當然。你要幾份？

Mr. Baker : A hundred and fifty. No, wait — make that a hundred and sixty.
    一百五十份，不，等等——印一百六十份好了。

Sandra : Yes, sir. Will there be anything else?
    好的，先生。還有其他的事嗎？

Mr. Baker : No thank you. That will be all for now.
    沒有了，謝謝。目前沒有別的事。

Sandra : Your copies will be ready in about ten minutes. 這份報告大約十分鐘就可以印好。

SUBSTITUTION DRILLS / 代換語句

1.

How many copies	would you like? do you need? do you prefer?

➡ 你需要影印幾份？

2.

Will there be Do you have Is there	anything else?

➡ 還有其他的事嗎？

3.

There is	a long line a long wait a lot of people	at the copy room.

➡ 影印室裏排了好多人。

4.

Which	paper size	should I use?

➡ 我應該用哪一種大小的紙張？

5.

Should I have it	bound or stapled? distributed? put in a folder?

➡ 我需不需要將它裝訂好還是用釘書機釘好／分送出去／放入檔案夾？

** bind〔baɪnd〕v. 裝訂（動詞三態是 bind, bound, bound）
staple〔'stepḷ〕v. 用釘書機釘起來
distribute〔dɪ'strɪbjʊt〕v. 分送

EXERCISE ／練習

● 模仿前面範例，完成下列對話。

Boss : _____ you copy this report for me?

Secretary : _____ . How many copies _____ ?

Boss : Please make _____ copies.

Secretary : _____ anything else?

Boss : That will be all for now.

Secretary : Your copies will be ready_____ .

KEY TO EXERCISE / 解答

1. Could, Certainly, would you like, a hundred and twenty, Will there be, in 5 minutes

2. Would, Of course, do you want, ten dozen, Is there, right away

A TIP FOR YOU / 秘書小點子

影印機上常用的標示符號

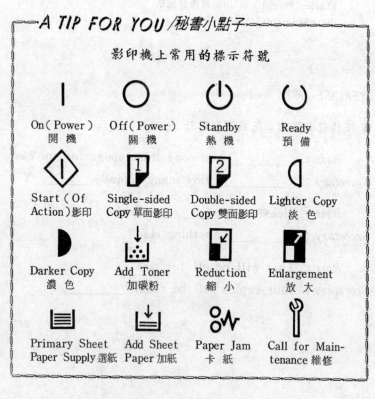

On（Power）
開機

Off（Power）
關機

Standby
熱機

Ready
預備

Start（Of Action）影印

Single-sided Copy 單面影印

Double-sided Copy 雙面影印

Lighter Copy
淡色

Darker Copy
濃色

Add Toner
加碳粉

Reduction
縮小

Enlargement
放大

Primary Sheet Paper Supply 選紙

Add Sheet Paper 加紙

Paper Jam
卡紙

Call for Maintenance 維修

UNIT 6 Dictation
聽寫

SAMPLE DIALOGUE / 實況對話

Mr. Baker : Sandra, I'd like to dictate a letter.
　　　　　　珊德拉，我要口述一封信。

Sandra : OK, sir. Please speak slowly. My shorthand isn't very good.
　　　　　好的，先生。請講慢一點。我的速記不是很好。

Mr. Baker : OK, ready? (Ahem) " Dear Sirs,... Perhaps you've forgotten about the money you owe me. However.... "
　　　　　　好了嗎?(啊哼)「敬啓者:⋯也許你已經忘了你欠我的錢了。不過⋯」

Sandra : Excuse me, sir.... 對不起，先生⋯

Mr. Baker : Yes, Sandra? 怎麼啦，珊德拉?

Sandra : You're speaking too quickly. 你講得太快了。

** dictate〔'dıktet〕*v.* 口述　shorthand〔'ʃɔrt,hænd〕*n.* 速記

SUBSTITUTION DRILLS /代換語句 ▨▨▨▨▨▨▨▨▨▨▨

1.

Please speak	slowly. clearly. loudly.

➡ 請講慢／清楚／大聲一點。

2.

Could you repeat the last	word? sentence? phrase?

➡ 你能重覆最後一個字／一句嗎？

3.

How do you spell that word? Would you spell that name please?

➡ 那個字怎麼拼？
　 請拼出那個名字好嗎？

4.

Correct me if	I am wrong. I don't get it right. I heard you wrong.

➡ 如果我聽錯了請糾正我。

5.

Let me just	read repeat	this to see if I got it right.

➡ 讓我讀／重覆一遍，看我有沒有寫錯。

EXERCISE / 練習

◉ 模仿前面範例，完成下列對話。

Boss : Sandra, I'd like to dictate a _____ .

Secretary : OK, sir. Please speak _____ . My _____ isn't very _____ .

Boss : OK, ready ?（Ahem）" _____ , _____ you've forgotten about the money you owe me. However.... "

Secretary : _____ , sir....

Boss : Yes, Sandra ?

Secretary : You're speaking too quickly.

KEY TO EXERCISE / 解答

1. letter, slowly, shorthand, good, Dear Sirs, Perhaps, Excuse me
2. fax, loudly, hearing, clear, Gentlemen, Possibly, Pardon me

UNIT 7 Reminders
提醒

SAMPLE DIALOGUE /實況對話

Sandra : You need to call your wife, Mr. Baker. She called at 10:00.

你必須打電話給你太太，貝克先生。她十點打電話來。

Mr. Baker : Thank you, Sandra. Are there any other messages? 謝謝妳，珊德拉。還有其他留言嗎？

Sandra : Oh yes, the marketing department called and asked you to lunch tomorrow.

喔，有。銷售部打電話來請你明天中午一起用餐。

Mr. Baker : I'll pencil them in. Will you get me their phone number?

我會記下來，妳能不能給我他們的電話號碼？

Sandra : Yes, sir. 好的，先生。

** message〔'mεsɪdʒ〕n. 留言　pencil〔'pɛnsl〕v. 用鉛筆寫

SUBSTITUTION DRILLS／代換語句

1.

You	need to call your wife.
	should call Mr. Williams back.
	must phone your mother-in-law.

➡ 你必須打電話給你太太／回電話給威廉斯先生／打電話給你岳母。

2.

Are there	
Do you have	any other messages?
Did I get	

➡ 還有其他的留言嗎？

3.

The marketing department	asked you to lunch tomorrow.
	wants to lunch with you to-morrow.

➡ 銷售部請你明天中午一起用餐。

4.

I'll	pencil them in.
	put them in my schedule.
	mark my calendar.

➡ 我會記下來／把它們排入時間表／在我的日曆上標明。

** calendar〔ˈkæləndə, ˈkælɪn-〕 n. 日曆

5.

Did you remember to pick up your	suit? dry-cleaning? laundry?

➡ 你記得拿你的西裝／送去乾洗的衣服／送洗的衣服了嗎？

EXERCISE ／練習

◉ 模仿前面範例，完成下列對話。

Secretary : You need to ＿＿＿＿＿＿ your wife, Mr. Wood.
 She called at noon.

 Boss : Thank you, Stella. Are there any other
 messages ?

Secretary : The ＿＿＿＿＿＿ department called and＿＿＿＿
 you to lunch tomorrow.

 Boss : I'll ＿＿＿＿＿＿. Will you get me their phone
 number ?

Secretary : Yes, sir.

KEY TO EXERCISE ／解答

1. call, marketing, asked, pencil them in
2. phone, accounting, invited, mark my calendar

Interpretation

翻譯

SAMPLE DIALOGUE / 實況對話

Mr. Baker : Mr. Lee, this is Sandra, my secretary. She'll be with us during the meeting.

李先生，這位是我的秘書珊德拉。會議進行時，她會和我們在一起。

Sandra : (in Chinese) I'm Sandra. It's nice to meet you, Mr. Lee. I'll be acting as your interpreter today.

（中文）我是珊德拉。很高興見到你，李先生。今天由我擔任你們的翻譯員。

Mr. Baker : Sandra, please tell Mr. Lee we're glad he could come today.

珊德拉，請告訴李先生我們很高興他今天能來。

Sandra : (in Chinese) We're so glad you can make it here today, Mr. Lee.

（中文）李先生，我們非常高興你能來。

SUBSTITUTION DRILLS /代換語句

1.
> I'm Sandra.
> I'm Mr. Baker's secretary, Sandra.
> My name is Sandra.

➡ 我是珊德拉。
　我是貝克先生的秘書珊德拉。
　我的名字叫珊德拉。

2.

It's	nice a pleasure good	to meet you, Mr. Lee.

➡ 李先生，很高興見到你。

3.

I'll be acting as I'll be I'm going to be	your interpreter today.

➡ 今天我將為你們翻譯。

4.

We're so glad	you can make it you are here you can come	today.

➡ 我們很高興你今天能來。

5. | It's a pleasure.
I'm glad to be here, too.
I've been looking forward to this meeting.

➡ 這是我的榮幸。
我也很高興能來這裏。
我一直期待著這次會議。

EXERCISE / 練習

◉ 模仿前面範例，完成下列對話。

> *Boss* : Mr. Wang, this is Angela, _____.
>
> *Secretary* : _____ , it's _____ to meet you, Mr.
> Wang. I'll be _____ today.
>
> *Boss* : Angela, please tell Mr. Wang, we're_____
> he could _____ today.
>
> *Secretary* : We're glad you could make it here today,
> Mr. Wang.

KEY TO EXERCISE / 解答

1. my secretary, I'm Angela, a pleasure, acting as your interpreter, happy, make it

2. She'll be our interpreter for today, My name is Angela, nice,
your interpreter, glad, be here

UNIT 9　Interruptions
打擾

I'm sorry to interrupt you.

SAMPLE DIALOGUE / 實況對話

Sandra : Mr. Baker, there is a Mr. Bush here to
　　　　see you. 貝克先生，有位布希先生要見你。

Mr. Baker : What does he want？ 他要做什麼？

Sandra : I'm not sure. I think he's selling something.
　　　　我不確定，我想他是要推銷東西。

Mr. Baker : I'm very busy. Please tell him I'm not here.
　　　　我很忙，請告訴他我不在。

Sandra : Yes, sir. 好的，先生。

Mr. Baker : Please see that I'm not interrupted again.
　　　　請注意別再讓任何事打擾我。

** see〔si〕v. 注意　interrupt〔͵ɪntəˋrʌpt〕v. 打擾

SUBSTITUTION DRILLS / 代換語句 ▓▓▓▓▓▓▓▓▓▓▓▓▓▓▓▓▓▓▓

1.

There's a Mr. Bush	here to see you. waiting to see you. on line 2.

➡ 有位布希先生要見你 / 等著見你 / 在二線 。

2.

I think he's It looks like he's It seems that he's	selling something.

➡ 我想他 / 他看起來 / 他好像是要推銷東西 。

3.

Excuse me, Can I have a minute, May I interrupt,	Mr. Baker. Mr. Baker?

➡ 抱歉，貝克先生 。
　　貝克先生，我能打擾一下嗎？

4.

He says	it's an emergency. it's important. it's urgent.

➡ 他說很緊急 / 有重要的事 / 有急事 。

** emergency〔ɪˈmɝdʒənsɪ〕n.緊急　urgent〔ˈɝdʒənt〕adj.緊急的

5.

The man insists	on seeing you.
	he has an appointment.
	he called you yesterday.

➡ 那個人堅持要見你／他事先有預約／他昨天打過電話給你。

6.

Should I	let him wait?
	ask him to come back?
	tell him to make another appointment?

➡ 我應該請他等會兒／請他再來／請他再約個時間嗎？

EXERCISE／練習

◉ 模仿前面範例，完成下列對話。

Secretary：Mr. Watson, there is a Mr. Bush _____.

Boss：What does he _____ ?

Secretary：I'm not _____. I think he's _____.

Boss：I'm busy. Please tell him I'm _____.

Secretary：Yes, sir.

Boss：Please _____ I'm not _____ again.

KEY TO EXERCISE / 解答

1. here to see you, want, sure, selling something, not here, see that, interrupted

2. calling, need, certain, a salesman, out, make sure, disturbed

—**A TIP FOR YOU** / 秘書小點子—

在上司與訪客洽談時，秘書若有要事必須稟告上司，應將該事項**寫在便條上**，敲門進入上司的辦公室後，**先向訪客道歉**，" I'm sorry to interrupt you." 再將便條交給上司，然後靜候一旁。退出時須**再度向訪客道歉**。便條的寫法如下：

Mr. Phillips of the AX Company:
He'd like to tell you something about the meeting the other day.
Would you like him to wait?

UNIT 16 Orders from the Boss
上司的指示

Which should I do frist?

SAMPLE DIALOGUE / 實況對話

Sandra : You buzzed, sir？先生，你叫我嗎？

Mr. Baker : Yes, I need you to take a letter, deliver this package and call my lawyer.

是的，我要妳寫一封信、寄這個包裹和打電話給我的律師。

Sandra : Yes, sir. Which would you like me to do first？

好的，先生。你要我先做哪一件事？

Mr. Baker : Please deliver the package first since it is the most urgent. Then call my lawyer, and then I'll be ready to dictate my letter.

包裹很緊急，所以先寄包裹。然後打電話給我的律師，之後我再來口述我的信。

Sandra : OK, sir. I will be back shortly. 好的，先生。我很快就回來。

** buzz〔bʌz〕v. 用呼叫器（buzzer）叫人　shortly〔ˈʃɔrtlɪ〕adv. 馬上

SUBSTITUTION DRILLS / 代換語句 ▨▨▨▨▨▨▨▨▨▨▨▨

1.

You	buzzed, rang, called,	sir ?

➡ 先生，你叫我嗎？

2.

Which	would you like do you want	me to do first?

➡ 你要我先做哪件事？

3.

I	will be back will return	shortly. soon. in a minute.

➡ 我很快就回來。

4.

Let me just	write jot note	that down.

➡ 讓我大略地記下來。

** ring〔rɪŋ〕*v.* 按鈴　　jot〔dʒɑt〕*v.* 略記

5.

I have	written it all down.
	memorized everything.
	everything in my notebook.

➡ 我已經全部寫下來了／記住了／記在筆記本裏了。

** memorize 〔'mɛmə,raɪz〕 v. 記憶

EXERCISE／練習

◉ 模仿前面範例，完成下列對話。

Secretary : You _____ , sir?

   Boss : Yes, I want you to take a letter, deliver this _____ , and call my _____ .

Secretary : Yes, sir. Which would you like me to do first?

   Boss : Please deliver the package first since it is the most _____ . Then call my lawyer, and then I'll be ready to dictate my letter.

Secretary : OK, sir. I will _____ .

   Boss : Please pick up _____ on your way back.

KEY TO EXERCISE／解答

1. buzzed, package, lawyer, urgent, be back shortly, some coffee

2. rang, document, lawyer, important, return soon, a pizza

UNIT 11 Office Problems
公司裏的問題

SAMPLE DIALOGUE / 實況對話

Sandra : Mr. Baker, there's a matter here that needs your attention. 貝克先生，有件事要提醒你注意。

Mr. Baker : What is it? 什麼事？

Sandra : We're having a little problem with our truck. 我們的貨車出了點問題。

Mr. Baker : What about it? 怎麼了？

Sandra : The engine needs to be overhauled. It keeps on breaking down on the road. 引擎需要徹底檢查，它在路上老是故障。

Mr. Baker : OK. Send the truck to the mechanic. 好，把貨車送去技工那裏。

** overhaul 〔‚ovəˈhɔl〕 v. 徹底檢查　　***keep on*** 不斷
break down 故障　　mechanic 〔məˈkænɪk〕 n. 技工

SUBSTITUTION DRILLS／代換語句 ═══════════════════════════════

1.

We're having a	little problem lot of trouble	with the truck.

➡ 我們的貨車出了一點／很多問題。

2.

The engine needs to be	checked. overhauled. repaired.

➡ 引擎需要檢查／徹底檢查／修理。

3.

It keeps on breaking down	on the road. during deliveries.

➡ 它在路上／在送貨時老是故障。

4.

The driver	has brought this up to me. has been complaining. has been in a lot of accidents.

➡ 司機告訴我這件事／不停地抱怨／已經出了很多次車禍。

＊＊ delivery〔dɪˈlɪvərɪ〕 n. 遞送；交貨　　　**bring up** 提出（問題）

5.

You've got to	do something about it.
	bring it to the mechanic.
	buy a new truck.

➡ 你應該想辦法解決／把它送去修理／買一輛新的貨車。

EXERCISE /練習

◉ 模仿前面範例，完成下列對話。

Secretary : Mr. Hawkins, there's a _____ here that needs your _____.

Boss : What is it ?

Secretary : We're having _____ with our truck.

Boss : What about it?

Secretary : The _____ needs to be _____. It keeps on breaking down _____.

Boss : OK, send the truck to the _____.

KEY TO EXERCISE /解答

1. problem, attention, a headache, truck, repaired, on the road, shop

2. matter, acting on, some trouble, engine, overhauled, during deliveries, mechanic

UNIT 12 Receiving a Fax

收傳眞

SAMPLE DIALOGUE ╱ 實況對話

Mr. Baker : Sandra, have we received the fax from ACME Company yet? 珊德拉，頂好公司的傳眞我們收到了嗎？

Sandra : Let me check…oh, here it is. It just arrived a few minutes ago. 我查一下…喔，在這裏。幾分鐘前剛到。

Mr. Baker : Excellent！ I've been expecting it.
好極了！我等很久了。

Sandra : Is it important? 這很重要嗎？

Mr. Baker : You bet it is. It's about the new contract.
當然啦！這和新合約有關。

Sandra : Here it is, sir. 就是這份，先生。

** fax〔fæks〕*n.* 無線電傳眞（= *facsimile*〔fæk'sɪmɪlɪ〕）
acme〔'ækmɪ〕*n.* 頂點　 *you bet* 當然

SUBSTITUTION DRILLS / 代換語句

1.

| Let me | check.
check on it.
have a look. |

➡ 讓我查一下。

2.

| Here it is,
Here you go,
I have it here, | sir. |

➡ 在這裏，先生。

3.

| The fax has been all | muddled.
garbled up. |

➡ 這份傳眞的字跡模糊不清。

4.

| I'll ask them to | send
transmit | another fax. |

➡ 我會請他們再傳眞一次。

** muddle〔'mʌdl̩〕v. 混亂　　garble〔'garbl̩〕v.(電稿等)不清楚
transmit〔træns'mɪt〕v. 傳送

5.

> They've only sent three pages.
> The other page is missing.
> They've missed out on the second page.

➡ 他們只傳了三頁。
　另一頁漏掉了。
　他們遺漏了第二頁。

6.

Should I	acknowledge receipt of this fax?
	call them that I've received the fax?
	send them a return fax?

➡ 我需不需要通知他們／打電話給他們／發傳眞給他們，說我們
　收到了傳眞？

** ***miss out*** 遺漏　acknowledge 〔ək'nɑlɪdʒ〕*v*.通知（已收到信件等）
receipt 〔rɪ'sit〕*n*. 接收

EXERCISE / 練習

◉ 模仿前面範例，完成下列對話。

Boss : Linda, have we＿＿＿＿ the fax from
ACME Company yet?

Secretary : Let me＿＿＿＿. Oh, here it is. It just
arrived a few minutes ago.

Boss : ＿＿＿＿＿＿ ! I've been ＿＿＿＿＿ it.

Secretary : Is it important ?

Boss : ＿＿＿＿＿ is. It's about the new ＿＿＿＿＿.

Secretary : ＿＿＿＿＿, Mr. Andersen.

KEY TO EXERCISE / 解答

1. received, have a look, Terrific, expecting, It sure, contract, Here it is

2. gotten, check, Great, waiting for, You bet it, agreement, Here you go

A TIP FOR YOU / 秘書小點子

傳眞機（ *fax machine* ）是現代國際貿易通訊中最進步的發明。它可以將文字、圖表、符號甚至照片等，以最快的速度傳送給對方，再加上**操作簡單**，因此成爲各公司不可或缺的裝置。需要注意的是，發**國際傳眞**時，如同撥國際電話，必須先撥本地國際冠碼（ international prefix ），與對方所在地國碼（ country code ），然後再撥對方的區域號碼（ area code ）與傳眞號碼。（ 參考 p.193 ）

UNIT 13 Faxing Someone
發傳眞

SAMPLE DIALOGUE／實況對話

Mr. Baker : Sandra, did you send the fax to Mr. Jones, yet？珊德拉，妳發傳眞給瓊斯先生了嗎？

Sandra : I tried, sir, but the fax line has been busy for the last ten minutes.
我試過了，先生，但是這十分鐘傳眞線路都佔線。

Mr. Baker : Why would it be busy for so long?
爲什麼會這麼久？

Sandra : Well, maybe it's because fax machines are so popular nowadays.
嗯，也許是因爲現在傳眞機太普遍了。

Mr. Baker : That's too bad. I really need to send that fax. 眞糟。我眞的急著發那份傳眞。

Sandra : I'll try again in five minutes.
五分鐘後我會再試試。

SUBSTITUTION DRILLS／代換語句 ▓▓▓▓▓▓▓▓▓▓▓▓▓▓

1.

I've already	sent relayed transmitted	the fax.

➡ 我已經發出傳眞了。

2.

The fax line has been	busy tied up	for the last ten minutes.

➡ 這十分鐘傳眞線路都佔線。

3.

I think	there's something wrong with their fax machine. their fax machine has broken down. their fax machine is out of order.

➡ 我想他們的傳眞機故障了。

4.

I will	fax try do it	again in five minutes.

➡ 五分鐘後我會再傳眞一次。

** relay〔rɪ'le, 'rile〕v. 轉送　　*tie up* 使不通
out of order 故障

5.

There's	a long line a long wait a lot of people	at the fax room.

➡ 傳眞室裏排了很多人。

EXERCISE / 練習

◉ 模仿前面範例,完成下列對話。

Boss : Martha, did you _____ the fax to Mr.
Jones, yet?

Secretary : I tried, sir, but the fax line has been _____
for the last ten minutes.

Boss : How can it be busy for such a long time?

Secretary : Well, _____ it's because fax machines
are _____ these days.

Boss : _____. I really need to send that fax.

Secretary : I'll try again in five minutes.

KEY TO EXERCISE / 解答

1. send, busy, perhaps, being used so much, Too bad

2. relay, tied up, maybe, so popular, What a shame

UNIT 14　Writing Memos
寫非正式信函

SAMPLE DIALOGUE／實況對話

Mr. Baker : Sandra, can you take a memo right now?
珊德拉，妳現在能寫封信嗎？

Sandra : No problem. I'm not very busy right now.
沒問題，我現在不忙。

Mr. Baker : Very good. It's to Mr. Lambert.
很好。是給藍伯特先生的。

Sandra : You mean Mr. Lambert from ACME Company?
你是說頂好公司的藍伯特先生？

Mr. Baker : That's right. He's waiting for my return fax.
對，他正在等我傳真過去。

Sandra : It sounds important. 聽起來很重要。

Mr. Baker : You bet. Let's get started.
當然。我們開始吧！

SUBSTITUTION DRILLS / 代換語句

1. | No problem.
   | Sure I can.
   | Yes, I can.
   | That's fine with me.

➡ 沒問題 / 當然好 。

2. | I'm not very busy | |
   | I'm not tied up | right now. |
   | I'm free | |

➡ 我現在不忙 / 有空 。

3. | | fix my position. |
   | Let me just | catch my breath for a minute. |
   | | get my notebook and pencil. |

➡ 讓我先坐好 / 喘一口氣 / 拿筆記本和筆 。

4. | | in a jiffy. |
   | I'll have it ready | in a moment. |
   | | in no time. |

➡ 我馬上準備好 。

** *catch one's breath* 喘一口氣　jiffy 〔ˋdʒɪfɪ〕 *n.* 一瞬間
   in no time 立刻

5.

Should I use the	letterhead?
	memo form?
	fax form?

➡ 我必須用公司的信紙／短箋的格式／傳眞的格式嗎？

** letterhead 〔'lɛtɚ‚hɛd〕 n. 印有信頭文字的信紙

EXERCISE／練習

◉ 模仿前面範例，完成下列對話。

　　Boss : Amelia, can you ＿＿＿＿＿ a memo right now?

Secretary : ＿＿＿＿＿. I'm not tied up ＿＿＿＿＿.

　　Boss : Great. ＿＿＿＿＿ to Mr. Lambert.

Secretary : You mean Mr. Lambert from ACME Company?

　　Boss : ＿＿＿＿＿. He's waiting for my return fax.

Secretary : It＿＿＿＿＿important.

　　Boss : You bet. Let's get started. " Dear Alfred, ＿＿＿＿＿ for the ＿＿＿＿＿ reply... "

KEY TO EXERCISE／解答 ▨▨▨▨▨▨▨▨▨▨▨

1. take , No problem, right now, It's, That's right, sounds, I'm sorry, late

2. write, Sure I can, at this moment, Address it, Exactly, seems, Excuse me, delayed

---

⌁A TIP FOR YOU／秘書小點子⌁

memorandum 通稱 **memo** ，是一種非正式信函。格式上省略了正式書信中的收信人地址、稱謂與信尾客套語，而由信紙上端開始寫：" *To* "接收信人（個人或團體），" *From* "接發信人，" *Date* "接發信日期，" *Subject* "接信文主旨，其下則以一般書信格式書寫內容。（參考 p. 229 ）

UNIT 15 Sending Greeting Cards
寄卡片

SAMPLE DIALOGUE / 實況對話

Mr. Baker : Sandra, have you finished writing all the Christmas cards?

珊德拉，所有的聖誕卡妳都寫完了嗎？

Sandra : Almost. You sure have a lot of customers, Mr. Baker. 差不多了。貝克先生，你的客戶可眞不少。

Mr. Baker : That's true. Sometimes it's hard to keep track of all of them.

這倒是眞的。有時很難和他們全部都保持聯繫。

Sandra : I'll be done with them sometime this morning. Is that OK? 我今天早上就可以寫完，這樣行嗎？

Mr. Baker : Fine. 很好。

** *keep track of* 與～保持聯繫

SUBSTITUTION DRILLS / 代換語句

1.
| Almost.
Just about. | You sure have | a lot of customers.
many clients. |

➡ 差不多了，你的客戶可真不少。

2.
| I'll be | done
finished
completed | with them sometime this morning. |

➡ 我今天早上就可以完成。

3.
| Should I put | the company seal
anything else | on these cards? |

➡ 要我在這些卡片上蓋公司的圖章／加其他的東西嗎？

4.
| Would you like to look at | the cards
the mailing list | before I mail them? |

➡ 在我寄之前你要不要看看這些卡片／這份郵寄名單？

** client 〔'klaɪənt〕 n. 客戶
seal 〔sil〕 n. 圖章

5.

I'll put the cards	on your desk. in your in-tray.

➡ 我會把這些卡片放在你桌上／放在收文架上。

6.

I need	to put stamps on your signature on you to sign	these cards.

➡ 這些卡片需要貼郵票／你的簽名／由你簽名。

** in-tray〔,ɪn'tre〕 n. （辦公室的）收文架
signature〔'sɪgnətʃæ〕 n. 簽名

EXERCISE ／練習

◉ 模仿前面範例，完成下列對話。

Boss : Alice, have you finished writing all the
Christmas cards ?

Secretary : _____. You_____ have many_____,
Mr. Arnold.

Boss : That's true. Sometimes it's _____ to
keep track of each one.

Secretary : I'll be _____with them sometime this
morning. Is that _____?

Boss : Fine.

KEY TO EXERCISE／解答

1. Almost, sure, customers, hard, finished, OK
2. Just about, really do, clients, difficult, done, fine

A TIP FOR YOU／秘書小點子

要使資料便於歸檔又便於取出，就必須做好檔案編排的工作。常用的檔案編排法有：㈠按**日期順序**排列。多用於訂單、帳單、發票及信件等檔案。㈡按**字母順序**排列。常用於以人名、公司名稱等歸檔時。人名要**先排姓，再排名**，例如：Judith R. White 排成 White, Judith R. 公司名稱則完全按照字母順序排列；若名稱中有數字，應將數字拼出，例如：7th Star Corporation 應排成 Seventh Star Corporation 。當然，如果能利用文書處理機（ word processor ）來存檔，那是再方便不過了。

UNIT 16 Sending Parcels and Packages
寄包裹

SAMPLE DIALOGUE / 實況對話

Mr. Baker : Sandra, is the parcel to ACME Co. ready to be sent? 珊德拉，寄給頂好公司的包裹準備好了嗎?

Sandra : Yes, it is. 好了。

Mr. Baker : Very good. They need it before Friday. 很好。他們星期五之前需要。

Sandra : Oh, in that case, we'll have to send it by air. 喔，如果是那樣的話，我們必須寄航空包裹。

Mr. Baker : Do whatever it takes. They've got to have it this week. 不管用什麼方法，他們這禮拜一定得收到。

Sandra : Don't worry, Mr. Baker. I'll take care of it right away. 別擔心，貝克先生。我會立刻處理的。

** parcel〔ˈpɑrsḷ〕*n.* 包裹

SUBSTITUTION DRILLS / 代換語句

1.

We'll	have need	to send it by	air. express.

➡ 我們必須空運／快遞。

2.

Surface mail takes	at least no less than about	a week.

➡ 普通郵件至少／大約要一個禮拜。

3.

It'll	get to reach arrive in	London next week.

➡ 下星期會到倫敦。

4.

I'll	take care of it carry it out	right away. at this moment.

➡ 我會立刻處理。

** express 〔ɪkˊsprɛs〕 n. 快遞　　*surface mail* 普通郵件
carry out 執行

5.

| This package is | to be sent to Argentina.
meant for the head office. |

➡ 這個包裹要寄往阿根廷／總公司。

6.

| We have | to buy some boxes.
to wrap these in brown paper.
a bunch of packages to send today. |

➡ 我們必須買些箱子／用牛皮紙包裝。
　我們今天有好幾宗包裹要寄。

** Argentina 〔ˌɑrdʒən'tinə〕 *n.* 阿根廷　　*head office* 總公司
brown paper 牛皮紙　　*a bunch of* 一綑

EXERCISE ／練習

◉ 模仿前面範例，完成下列對話。

Boss : Karen, is the package ready to be _____ ?

Secretary : _____ , it is.

Boss : Excellent. They _____ it before Friday.

Secretary : Oh, in that case, we'll need to send it by _____ .

Boss : Do whatever it takes. They _____ it this week.

Secretary : Don't worry, Mr. Adams. I'll _____
immediately.

KEY TO EXERCISE / 解答 ▓▓▓▓▓▓▓▓▓▓▓▓▓▓▓▓▓▓

1. sent, Yes, must have, air, need, take care of it
2. delivered, Sure, must receive, express, should have, carry it out

國際 & 國內包裹資費表

(1)普通資費

水　陸　函　件　資　費			香　港澳　　門	國　外　其他　各　地
	計　費　標　準			
國際包裹	不逾 100 公克		10.00	21.00
	逾 100 公克　不逾 250 公克		20.00	38.00
	逾 250 公克　不逾 500 公克		35.00	69.00
	逾 500 公克　不逾 1000 公克		57.00	114.00
	逾1000 公克　不逾 2000 公克		81.00	160.00

航空函件資費（水陸及航空混合）		香　港澳　　門	亞　洲　及大　洋　洲	歐非中南美洲各地	美　　國加　拿　大
	計費標準				
國際包裹	不逾 20 公克	7.00	10.00	13.00	13.00
	每續重20公克	5.00	7.00	10.00	10.00
國內包裹	（每件限重不逾一公斤）每重 100 公克 10.00 元				

(2)特種資費

國 際			國 內		
類 別	計費標準	資 費	類 別	計 費 標 準	資 費
掛號費	每件另加	24.00	航 空 費	每重20公克另加	2.00
			掛 號 費	每件另加	14.00
快遞費	每件另加	30.00	限時專送費	每件另加	7.00

UNIT 17 Speed Delivery
寄限時包裹

SAMPLE DIALOGUE / 實況對話

Mr. Baker : Sandra, can you send this package by speed delivery for me?
珊德拉，妳能不能替我寄這個限時包裹？

Sandra : OK. Do you want it registered? 好。要寄掛號嗎？

Mr. Baker : Should it be registered? 有必要掛號嗎？

Sandra : Well, just to be on the safe side, I don't think it's a bad idea.
呃，爲了安全起見，我覺得掛號也好。

Mr. Baker : How much is it going to cost? 郵資是多少？

Sandra : I'll call the post office now and find out.
我現在就打電話問郵局。

** *speed delivery* 限時專送　register 〔'rɛdʒɪstə〕 v. 將(郵件)掛號
on the safe side 以防萬一

SUBSTITUTION DRILLS / 代換語句

1.

We have to send the package	before the end of July. before the New Year holidays. immediately.

➡ 我們必須在七月底以前／在新年以前／立刻寄出包裹。

2.

I'll	call get in touch with	the post office now and	make sure. find out.

➡ 我現在就打電話／聯絡郵局以便確定。

3.

Speed delivery will	cost more. be more expensive. get it there faster.

➡ 寄限時較貴／快。

4.

Do you want it registered ?   Would you like it registered ?

➡ 你要寄掛號嗎？

**　get in touch with** 和～聯絡

5.

| The package is | too heavy.
too big. |

➡ 郵包過重／過大。

EXERCISE／練習

◉ 模仿前面範例，完成下列對話。

Boss : Lisa, can you ＿＿＿＿ this parcel by＿＿＿＿
　　　　 delivery for me?

Secretary : OK.＿＿＿＿it registered?

Boss : Should it be registered?

Secretary : Well, just to be on the safe side, I don't
　　　　　　 think it's a bad idea.

Boss : ＿＿＿＿is it going to cost?

Secretary : I'll ＿＿＿＿the post office now and
　　　　　　 ＿＿＿＿.

KEY TO EXERCISE／解答

1. send, speed, Do you want, How much, call, find out

2. ship, express, Would you like, What, get in touch with, make
sure

UNIT 18　The Beeper
以呼叫器叫人

SAMPLE DIALOGUE / 實況對話

Mr. Baker : Please call security. 請叫警衛。

Sandra : OK, I will page them on their beeper.
好，我用呼叫器來叫他們。

Mr. Baker : Please tell them I need to file a report on the broken lock on my office door.
請告訴他們我辦公室的門鎖被人破壞，我要報案。

Sandra : Yes, sir. They will get the message shortly.
好的，先生。他們很快就會收到消息。

Mr. Baker : Tell them how it happened. 告訴他們事情的經過。

Sandra : Consider it done, sir. 一切照你的吩咐，先生。

** security〔sɪ'kjʊrətɪ〕*n.* 警衛　　page〔pedʒ〕*v.* 喊要找的人
beeper〔'bipɚ〕*n.* 呼叫器　　file〔faɪl〕*v.* 提出（陳情等）

SUBSTITUTION DRILLS／代換語句 ▨▨▨▨▨▨▨▨▨▨

1.

I will	page them beep them	on their beeper.

➡ 我用呼叫器來叫他們。

2.

I'd like to file a report on	a broken window. a stolen computer. a missing file.

➡ 我的窗戶遭人破壞／電腦失竊／檔案失竊，我要報案。

3.

They will	get the message answer their page beep back	shortly.

➡ 他們很快就會得到消息／回答／用呼叫器回答。

4.

Consider it done, Of course, No problem,	sir.

➡ 照你的吩咐／當然／沒問題，先生。

5. He is	still on the streets. taking his vacation. at a meeting.

➡ 他還在街上／在度假／在開會。

6. He has a	pager beeper	with him.

➡ 他帶著呼叫器。

EXERCISE ／ 練習

◉ 模仿前面範例，完成下列對話。

Boss : Please_____security.

Secretary : OK, I will_____them on their beeper.

Boss : Please tell them I need to_____a report on a broken_____on my office door.

Secretary : Yes, sir. They will_____shortly.

Boss : Tell them_____, please.

Secretary : _____, sir.

KEY TO EXERCISE /解答 ░░░░░░░░░░░░░░░░░░░░░░░░

1. call, page, file, lock, get the message, how it happened,
   Consider it done

2. contact, call, make, knob, answer back, the circumstances,
   No problem

──A TIP FOR YOU /秘書小點子──

呼叫器（ beeper，俗稱 *BB call* ）的體積小，攜帶非常
方便。每個呼叫器都有一個號碼，有事找攜帶者就用**電
話**撥呼叫器的號碼，呼叫器即**發出嗶嗶的聲音**。呼叫器
無法直接通話，但會顯示出發訊者的資料，攜帶者接到
訊號後再與發訊者聯絡。

UNIT 19　Reporting Activities
報告會議過程

SAMPLE DIALOGUE／實況對話

Sandra : Inside you'll find the minutes of the meeting.
會議的紀錄在這裏面。

Mr. Baker : How long did the meeting last? 會議進行了多久?

Sandra : It lasted for three hours. There were some
very heated discussions.
三個小時。有幾項討論相當熱烈。

Mr. Baker : Did they ask for me? 他們有沒有問起我?

Sandra : No, but I think you'll have to do some follow-
ups. 沒有。不過我想你必須做些後續工作。

Mr. Baker : Alright, Sandra. I'll call you back if I have
any questions. 好,珊德拉。我有問題再叫妳。

** minutes〔'mɪnɪts〕*n. pl.* 會議紀錄　heated〔'hitɪd〕*adj.* 熱烈的
follow-up〔'falo,ʌp〕*n.* 緊接的行動

SUBSTITUTION DRILLS／代換語句 ▨▨▨▨▨▨▨▨▨▨▨

1.

Inside you'll find	what transpired at the minutes of a summary of what happened in	the meeting.

➡ 會議的紀錄在這裏面。

2.

The meeting	lasted for three hours. was delayed by 30 minutes. was well attended.

➡ 會議進行了三個小時／遲了三十分鐘才開始／出席的情況良好。

3.

The chairman asked for you. I explained to them that you couldn't make it. Some of the managers asked why you couldn't come.

➡ 主席問起你。
　我向他們說明你無法出席。
　有幾位經理問你無法出席的原因。

** transpire 〔træn'spaɪr〕 v. 發生
summary 〔'sʌmərɪ〕 n. 摘要　　attend 〔ə'tɛnd〕 v. 出席；參加

4.

I have	a recording of the meeting. the transcripts of the meeting. all the reports and materials handed out in the meeting.

➡ 我有會議的錄音／會議紀錄／會議中所發的報告和資料。

5.

I think you have to	do some follow-ups. make some phone-calls. submit some replies.

➡ 我想你必須做些後續工作／打些電話／做些回答。

** transcript〔'træn,skrɪpt〕 n.（演說等的）筆記
hand out 分發　　submit〔səb'mɪt〕 v. 提出

EXERCISE／練習

◉ 模仿前面範例，完成下列對話。

Secretary： Inside you'll find _____ the meeting.

　　Boss： How long did the meeting _____?

Secretary： It _____.

　　Boss： Did they ask _____ me?

Secretary： No, but I think you'll have to _____.

　　Boss： Alright, Sandra. I'll call you back if

　　　　　_____.

KEY TO EXERCISE /解答 ░░░░░░░░░░░░░░░░░░░░░░░░░░░░

1. the minutes of, take, took them only 3 hours, for, make some phone calls, there is anything here I don't understand

2. a summary of what happened in, last, lasted for 3 hours, about, do some follow-ups, I have any questions

┌───┐
│   │
│ ─A TIP FOR YOU /秘書小點子─   │
│   │
│   秘書有時必須為客戶與上司的會談做翻譯。通常是由上   │
│ 司或客戶說一個段落後停下來，秘書接著轉譯，這種稱   │
│ 為**連續翻譯**（ *consecutive interpretation* ）。秘書平 │
│ 時應該多**訓練聽力**與**記憶力**，才能做好翻譯的工作；在   │
│ 翻譯時，必須注意聽說話者的每一句話，並適時利用**速**   │
│ **記**來幫助記憶。   │
│   │
└───┘

UNIT 20 Preparing the Itinerary
安排行程

SAMPLE DIALOGUE / 實況對話

Mr. Baker : Alright. Give me a run-down of my itinerary.

好吧，大略報告一下我的行程。

Sandra : You'll arrive at Heathrow Airport on June 1 and I've booked you at the Ambassador Hotel near the town center. On the next day, you'll have your meeting with Mr. Bell and the day after that will be the convention. You'll have a day for shopping and sightseeing. Then your flight back home is on June 5.

六月一號你會飛抵希斯羅機場，我已經爲你訂了市中心附近的國賓飯店。第二天，你要與貝爾先生會面，第三天就是會議舉行的日子。然後你有一天的時間觀光購物，六月五號搭機回國。

** run-down〔'rʌn,daʊn〕n. 概要報告
itinerary〔aɪ'tɪnə,rɛrɪ, ɪ-〕n. 旅程　book〔bʊk〕v. 預訂
ambassador〔æm'bæsədə〕n. 大使

SUBSTITUTION DRILLS / 代換語句

1.

This is a	brief run-down summary tentative listing	of your itinerary.

➡ 這是關於你行程的簡短報告／摘要／暫定計畫。

2.

You'll arrive	at Heathrow Airport in London at your destination	on June 1.

➡ 你將於六月一號飛抵希斯羅機場／倫敦／目的地。

3.

I've booked you I've made reservations You're staying	at the Ambassador Hotel.

➡ 我已經為你訂了／你將投宿國賓飯店。

4.

The hotel is near	the town center. the convention center. the airport.

➡ 那家飯店靠近市中心／會議中心／機場。

** convention 〔kən'vɛnʃən〕 n. 會議　tentative〔'tɛntətɪv〕adj.暫時的
destination 〔,dɛstə'neʃən〕 n. 目的地

5.

You'll have your meeting You're scheduled to meet I've arranged an appointment	with Mr. Bell the next day.

➡ 隔天你要與貝爾先生會面。

EXERCISE ╱*練習*

◉ 模仿前面範例，完成下列對話。

> *Boss* : Alright, give me a _____ of my itinerary.
>
> *Secretary* : You'll arrive_____ on June 1 and_____
> at the Ambassador Hotel. The hotel is near
> the_____. On the next day_____
> Mr. Marwick, and then_____will be the
> convention. You'll have a day for_____.
> Then your_____is on June 5.

KEY TO EXERCISE ╱*解答*

1. brief run-down, in London, I've booked you, town center,
   you'll have your meeting with, the following, rest, departure
   date

2. summary, at Heathrow Airport, I've made reservations,
   convention center, you're scheduled to see, the day after,
   sightseeing, flight back home

UNIT  **21** **Post-Trip Follow-Ups**

業務旅行後的工作

SAMPLE DIALOGUE / 實況對話 ▨▨▨▨▨▨▨▨▨▨

Sandra : Mr. Baker, would you like me to put the
calling cards on your name card album?

貝克先生，你要不要我把這些名片收進你的名片簿裏？

Mr. Baker : By all means. Here they are. This is a list
of my expenses during the trip.

當然，在這裏。這張單子列著我這次旅行的開銷。

Sandra : Is there anyone you would like to write to?

你有沒有要寫信給誰？

Mr. Baker : Yes. Write to Mr. Denver thanking him for
his hospitality.

有。寫給丹佛先生，感謝他的慇懃招待。

** ***by all means*** 當然　　expense〔ɪksˈpɛns〕*n.* 開支；費用
hospitality〔͵hɑspɪˈtælətɪ〕*n.* 慇懃款待

SUBSTITUTION DRILLS / 代換語句

1.

Would you like me to put the cards on your	name card album? electronic diary ?

➡ 你要不要我把這些名片收進你的名片簿／電子日記裏？

2.

Do you have the	expense report of receipts for expense breakdown of	your trip ?

➡ 你有這次旅行的開銷紀錄／收據／開支明細表嗎？

3.

Is there anyone you would like to	write to ? thank ? communicate with ?

➡ 你有沒有要寫信給誰／感謝誰／聯絡誰？

4.

Do you want me to	compose write draft	the letter myself ?

➡ 你要我自己來寫這封信嗎？

** receipt〔rɪ'sit〕 n. 收據　breakdown〔'brek,daʊn〕 n. 細目
compose〔kəm'poz〕v.作(詩、文等)　draft〔dræft〕v. 起草

5.

| Would you like | to dictate the letter to me?
to do the dictation now?
to tell me the outline of the letter? |

➡ 你想口述這封信／現在口述／告訴我這封信的大綱嗎？

＊＊ outline 〔'aʊt,laɪn〕 *n.* 大綱

EXERCISE ∕練習

◉ 模仿前面範例，完成下列對話。

Secretary : Would you like me to put the cards on your
_____ ?

Boss : By all means. Here they are. This is the
_____ my trip.

Secretary : Is there anyone you would like to _____ ?

Boss : Yes. Write to Mr. Locke thanking him for
his _____ and another one to Mr. Sullivan
telling him we'll be _____ with him as
soon as our lawyers go over his proposal.

KEY TO EXERCISE ∕解答

1. Rolodex, expense list of, thank, assistance, communicating

2. electronic diary, expense breakdown of, write to, hospitality,
getting in touch

UNIT **22　Ordering Lunch**
訂購午餐

SAMPLE DIALOGUE / 實況對話 ⬚⬚⬚⬚⬚⬚⬚⬚⬚

Mr. Baker : Sandra, we will be in this meeting longer than planned. Please order some take-out pizza for our lunch.

珊德拉，這次會議會比預訂的時間長。請訂一些外帶的比薩做午餐。

Sandra : For how many people？要多少人份？

Mr. Baker : There are twelve of us. 共十二位。

Sandra : Alright... I'll call over to Pizza Hut and place the order right away.

好…我立刻就打電話向「必勝客」訂購。

**　take-out〔'tek,aʊt〕*adj.*（餐點等）供外帶的
　　pizza〔'pitsə〕*n.* 比薩；義大利脆餅

SUBSTITUTION DRILLS / 代換語句 ▨▨▨▨▨▨▨▨▨▨▨▨▨▨▨

1.

We will	be in prolong	this meeting longer than	usual. planned. scheduled.

➡ 這次會議會比平常/預定久些。

2.

There are	twelve a dozen	of us.

➡ 共十二位。

3.

Would you like Do you want	me to order anything	extra ? else ? to drink?

➡ 你要我再叫些其他的/飲料嗎?

4.

We'll need	a dozen cups. twelve plates. a large pot of hot coffee.

➡ 我們要十二人份/一大壺熱咖啡。

** prolong〔prəˈlɔŋ,-ˈlɑŋ〕v. 延長　extra〔ˈɛkstrə〕adj. 額外的
plate〔plet〕n. 一人份　　pot〔pɑt〕n. 壺

5.

I'll call over to	Chef Wang's the restaurant	and	place tell them	the order.

➡ 我會打電話到王厨／餐廳訂購。

** chef 〔ʃɛf〕 *n.* 主厨

EXERCISE ／練習

◉ 模仿前面範例，完成下列對話。

Boss : Susan, we will_____this meeting longer than_____. Please order some take-out Chinese food for our lunch.

Secretary : For how many people?

Boss : There are_____of us.

Secretary : _____ me to_____anything else?

Boss : We'll need a round of soft drinks.

Secretary : Alright... I'll call over to_____and _____ the order now.

KEY TO EXERCISE ／解答

1. be in, planned, a dozen, Would you like, get you, the cafeteria, tell them

2. prolong, usual, twelve, Do you want, order, Chef Wang's, place

UNIT 23 Running Personal Errands
辦私事

SAMPLE DIALOGUE / 實況對話 ░░░░░░░░░

Sandra : Mr. Baker, will you watch my desk for me?
貝克先生，幫我看一下桌子好嗎？

Mr. Baker : Sure, Sandra. Where are you going?
好啊，珊德拉。妳要去哪裏？

Sandra : I have to go pick up my laundry from the dry cleaners on the corner. 我要去轉角的乾洗店拿衣服。

Mr. Baker : Will you be gone very long? 妳要去很久嗎？

Sandra : No, only about ten minutes. Can I get you something? 不，大約只去十分鐘。要我替你帶點東西嗎？

Mr. Baker : No, thanks. 不必了，謝謝。

** laundry 〔ˈlɔndrɪ, ˈlɑn-〕 n. 送洗的衣物
dry cleaner 乾洗店

SUBSTITUTION DRILLS / 代換語句

1.

Will you watch my	desk office telephone	for me?

➡ 你能替我看一下桌子 / 看一下辦公室 / 接電話嗎 ?

2.

I'm going to	pick up your coat from the dry cleaners. get my laundry from the laundromat. do some shopping.

➡ 我要去乾洗店拿你的外套 。
我要去自助洗衣店拿我的衣服 。
我要去買點東西 。

3.

I won't be gone	a long time. very long. a long while.

➡ 我不會去很久 。

4.

No, only	a few minutes. a little while. a couple of minutes.

➡ 不 , 只去幾分鐘 。

** laundromat 〔ˋlɔndrəmæt〕 *n.* 自助洗衣店　　*a couple of* 幾個 ; 數個

5.

Can I	buy get bring	you something ?

➡ 要我替你買／帶點東西嗎？

EXERCISE／練習

◉模仿前面範例，完成下列對話。

Secretary : Mr. Patterson,＿＿＿＿＿my desk for me?

Boss : Sure, Janet.＿＿＿＿＿?

Secretary : I have to go＿＿＿＿＿.

Boss : Will you be gone very long?

Secretary : No, only＿＿＿＿＿. Can I＿＿＿＿＿?

Boss : ＿＿＿＿＿.

KEY TO EXERCISE／解答

1. will you watch, Where are you going, pick up my laundry,
   a few minutes, get you something, If you wouldn't mind

2. could you stay at, What do you need to do, do some shopping,
   about half an hour, do an errand for you, No thanks

UNIT 24　**Requests**
要求

SAMPLE DIALOGUE / 實況對話

Sandra : May I come in? 我可以進來嗎?

Mr. Baker : Come in! What do you want? 請進，有什麼事?

Sandra : Mr. Baker, you know I've been working here for six years. 貝克先生,你知道我在這裏已經工作六年了。

Mr. Baker : Yes? 然後呢?

Sandra : I think I deserve a raise. 我想我應該加薪。

Mr. Baker : But you are late almost every day.
但是妳幾乎每天遲到。

Sandra : I can't afford to buy a car. 我買不起車子嘛!

Mr. Baker : I'll think about it. 我會考慮的。

** deserve 〔dɪˈzɝv〕 v. 應得　　raise 〔rez〕 n. 加薪
afford 〔əˈford〕 v. 力足以~

SUBSTITUTION DRILLS /代換語句

1.

Can I	have a minute? come in ? · talk to you?

➡ 我可以打擾一下／進來／和你說幾句話嗎？

2.

I think it's time	I got a raise. to buy a new typewriter.

➡ 我想是該加薪／買新打字機的時候了。

3.

I'd like to	do a better job. switch jobs. be recognized for my contributions.

➡ 我希望做得更好／換工作／我的貢獻受到肯定。

4.

I could really do a lot better with	an assistant. a better seat. a computer.

➡ 如果有一位助手／一個較好的座位／一台電腦，我會做得更好。

** switch 〔swɪtʃ〕 v. 轉換　recognize 〔'rɛkəg,naɪz〕 v. 肯定
contribution 〔,kɑntrə'bjuʃən〕 n. 貢獻

5.

| If it's | not asking to much.
alright with you.
within your budget. |

➡ 如果要求不算過分／你覺得可以／在你預算之內。

** budget〔ˈbʌdʒɪt〕n. 預算

EXERCISE／練習

◉ 模仿前面範例，完成下列對話。

Boss : Come in! What do you _____?

Secretary : You know I've been working here for_____.

Boss : _____?

Secretary : I_____ I_____ a raise.

Boss : But you are late_____every day.

Secretary : I can't afford to_____a car.

Boss : I'll_____it.

KEY TO EXERCISE／解答

1. want, six years, Yes, think, deserve, almost, buy, think about

2. need, a long time, And...., believe, should get, nearly, purchase, consider

UNIT 25 Apologies
道歉

SAMPLE DIALOGUE ╱ 實況對話

Mr. Baker : You're twenty minutes late today.
　　　　　　妳今天遲到二十分鐘。

　Sandra : I'm sorry. I missed the bus. 很抱歉,我錯過了公車。

Mr. Baker : This is the third time this week.
　　　　　　這已經是這禮拜的第三次了。

　Sandra : I promise it won't happen again.
　　　　　　我保證以後不會再遲到。

Mr. Baker : You're fired! 妳被解雇了!
　Sandra : Please don't fire me! 請不要開除我!

Mr. Baker : I'm only joking. 我只是在開玩笑。

　** fire〔faɪr〕v. 解雇　　joke〔dʒok〕v. 開玩笑

SUBSTITUTION DRILLS / 代換語句

1.

I'm sorry. I	missed the bus. missed the train. lost my car keys.

➡ 很抱歉，我錯過了公車／錯過了火車／弄丟了汽車鑰匙。

2.

I promise	it won't happen again. I won't do it again. this will be the last time.

➡ 我保證以後不會再發生／不會再犯／這是最後一次。

3.

I'll do overtime today I'll work extra hard	to make up for the lost time.

➡ 我今天會加班／格外努力，來彌補少做的時間。

4.

I tried my best. I did all I could. I gave it my best shot.

➡ 我已經盡力了。

** overtime〔'ovɚ,taɪm〕 adv. 超出時間地
   extra〔'ɛkstrə〕 adv. 特別地   shot〔ʃɑt〕 n. 嘗試

5.

> It's really my fault.
> The blame is on me.
> I'm responsible for this.

➡ 的確是我的錯。
　我應該受責難。
　我應該為這件事負責。

6.

Could you give me	another chance ?
	some more time to adjust?
	some advice?

➡ 你能不能再給我一次機會／一些時間適應／一些建議？

＊＊ blame〔blem〕n. 責難　　adjust〔ə'dʒʌst〕v. 適應

EXERCISE ╱ 練習

◉ 模仿前面範例，完成下列對話。

　　Boss : You're＿＿＿＿late today.
Secretary : I missed the＿＿＿＿.

　　Boss : This is the＿＿＿＿time this＿＿＿＿.
Secretary : I promise it won't happen again.

　　Boss : You're＿＿＿＿!
Secretary : Please don't fire me !

　　Boss : I'm only＿＿＿＿.

KEY TO EXERCISE / 解答

1. twenty minutes, bus, third, week, fired, joking
2. over 2 hours, train, fourth, month, terminated, kidding

A TIP FOR YOU / 秘書小點子

要為上司安排成功的國外業務旅行，事前必須做周詳的計畫。旅行所需的證件、機票以及投宿旅館，可請熟悉的**旅行社代辦**，不過要先問清楚上司的喜好，例如上司喜歡頭等艙還是經濟艙，要住普通房間還是高級套房等。行程的安排**不要過於緊湊**，各地時差、班機延誤等因素都必須列入考慮。行程表（*itinerary*）草擬之後，要**與上司逐項核對**，一切底定後，準備二份，一份交由上司隨身攜帶，一份由秘書自己保留，以便有緊急情況時，可以聯絡上。（參考 p. 136）

UNIT 26 **Taking a Leave**
請假

SAMPLE DIALOGUE / 實況對話

Sandra : Mr. Baker, can I talk to you?
　　　　　貝克先生，我能跟你談談嗎？

Mr. Baker : What's the matter? 什麼事？

Sandra : I have a problem. I can't be here to sort the mail this afternoon.
　　　　　我有一個問題，我今天下午不能在這裏整理郵件。

Mr. Baker : Why not? 為什麼不能？

Sandra : I have a doctor's appointment. 我和醫生有約。

Mr. Baker : Okay. I will find someone else to do it.
　　　　　好，我會找人代做。

** sort〔sɔrt〕*v*. 分類整理

SUBSTITUTION DRILLS / 代換語句

1.

I have to	take a few days off. leave for a few days.

➡ 我必須請假幾天。

2.

I have some things to	take care of. do. solve.

➡ 我有些事情要處理/做/解決。

3.

I can't be here to	sort the mail answer the telephone type letters	this afternoon.

➡ 我今天下午不能在這裏整理郵件/接電話/打字。

4.

I have a	doctor's dentist's beauty shop	appointment.

➡ 我和醫生/牙醫/美容院有約。

** dentist〔'dɛntɪst〕 n. 牙醫

5.

Can you find	someone else another person another secretary	to do it?

➡ 你能不能找人／其他秘書代做？

EXERCISE / 練習 ▨▨▨▨▨▨▨▨▨▨▨▨▨

◉ 模仿前面範例，完成下列對話。

Secretary : Mr. James,＿＿＿＿＿ you ?

　　Boss : ＿＿＿＿＿ ?

Secretary : I have a problem. I can't be here to＿＿＿＿
　　　　　 this afternoon.

　　Boss : Why＿＿＿＿＿ ?

Secretary : I have＿＿＿＿＿ .

　　Boss : Okay. I will＿＿＿＿＿ .

KEY TO EXERCISE / 解答 ▨▨▨▨▨▨▨▨▨▨▨▨▨

1. can I talk to, What's the matter, answer the telephone, not, a doctor's appointment, find someone else to do it

2. may I see, What do you want, work, can't you, to go somewhere, get another secretary

CHAPTER 2

Communications with Various Publics

與外界交際

UNIT 1　At the Reception Desk
在櫃台

SAMPLE DIALOGUE / 實況對話

Sandra : Hello. How can I help you? 嗨，我能幫上忙嗎？

Salesperson : Good morning. I'm from ACME Office Supply Company. 早安，我是頂好辦公用品公司的人。

Sandra : Do you have an appointment with someone? 你和誰有約嗎？

Salesperson : Yes. I have one with Mr. Baker at 10:15. 是的，我和貝克先生約十點十五分。

Sandra : Please have a seat. I'll check to make sure he's in. 請坐。我來看看貝克先生在不在。

Salesperson : I'd appreciate that. 謝謝。

** appreciate〔ə'priʃɪ,et〕 *v.* 感謝

SUBSTITUTION DRILLS / 代換語句

1.

Hello.	How can I help What can I do for Can I be of assistance to	you?

➡ 嗨，需要我幫忙嗎？

2.

Do you have	an appointment a meeting scheduled	with someone?

➡ 你和誰約要見面嗎？

3.

Please	have a seat. sit down over there. wait a minute.

➡ 請坐／請那邊坐／請等一下。

4.

I'll	check go see	to make sure he's in.

➡ 我去看看他在不在。

** assistance〔ə'sɪstəns〕n. 幫助

5.

Can I have your	calling card? visiting card? card?

➡ 能不能給我你的名片 ？

6.

You're	a little bit late. early for your appointment. just in luck. He's free to see you.

➡ 你遲了一點 。

你比約定時間早到。

你來得正好，他現在有空見你。

** *in luck* 運氣好

EXERCISE / 練習

◉ 模仿前面範例，完成下列對話 。

Secretary : _____. _____I help you ?

Visitor : _____. _____ACME Office Supply

Company.

Secretary : Do you have an appointment with_____ ?

Visitor : Yes. I have one with Mr. Edwards at 10:15.

Secretary : Please＿＿＿＿a seat. I'll check to make
　　　　　sure＿＿＿＿.

　Visitor : I'd appreciate that.

KEY TO EXERCISE /解答

1. Hello, How can, Good morning, I'm from, my boss, take,
   he's in

2. Good morning, Can, Yes, I represent, someone, have, you're
   scheduled

A TIP FOR YOU /秘書小點子

有預約的訪客到達時，**先通知上司一聲**，再引他進上司
的辦公室。若訪客比預定的時間早到，而上司又正在處
理其他的事，則可安排訪客至會客室等候。

UNIT 2 In the Reception Room
在會客室

SAMPLE DIALOGUE/ 實況對話

Sandra : Please have a seat, Mr. Brown.
Mr. Baker will be along shortly.
請坐，布朗先生。貝克先生馬上就來。

Mr. Brown : Thank you. 謝謝妳。

Sandra : Would you like something to drink, coffee
or black tea？ 您要不要喝點什麼，咖啡還是紅茶？

Mr. Brown: Yes, I'd like some coffee, please.
好，請給我咖啡。

Sandra : Cream and sugar？ 要加奶精和糖嗎？

Mr. Brown : Just sugar, please. 加糖就好，謝謝。

** be along 會來　　shortly〔'ʃɔrtlɪ〕adv. 馬上；不久

SUBSTITUTION DRILLS/代換語句

1.

| Please | have a seat,
sit down,
be seated,
take a seat, | Mr. Brown. |

➡ 請坐，布朗先生。

2.

| Mr. Baker
He
She | will be | along shortly.
here soon.
right with you. |

➡ 貝克先生／他／她馬上就來。

3.

| Would you like something | to drink?
to eat? |

➡ 你要不要喝／吃點什麼？

4.

| Would you like some | coffee?
tea?
green tea? |

➡ 你要不要來點咖啡／茶／綠茶？

5.

| Would you like | tea or coffee? |
| | cream and sugar? |

➡ 你要茶還是咖啡？
你要加奶精和糖嗎？

6.

I'd like	some coffee,	please.
	a cup of coffee,	
	some tea,	
	a cup of tea,	

➡ 請給我咖啡／一杯咖啡／茶／一杯茶。

EXERCISE / 練習

◉ 模仿前面範例，完成下列對話。

Secretary : Please _____ a seat, _____.
The sales manager will be _____.

Visitor : Thank you.

Secretary : Would you like _____ to _____,
coffee or green tea?

Visitor : Yes, I'd like some _____, please.

Secretary : Cream and sugar?

Visitor : Just _____, please.

KEY TO EXERCISE / 解答

1. have, Mr. Jones, along shortly, something, drink, coffee, sugar

2. take, Miss Marks, here soon, something, drink, coffee, black

---

A TIP FOR YOU / 秘書小點子

有客來訪,應徵詢對方要喝茶或咖啡,並問明是否加糖或奶精。訪客在等待時,秘書應**注意其情緒反應**,若發覺對方等得不耐煩,可以帶他參觀辦公室或陪他聊聊;若是沒空,別忘了準備書刊報紙等,讓訪客消磨時間。

UNIT 3　A Visitor a Secretary Knows Well
秘書熟識的訪客

SAMPLE DIALOGUE／實況對話

Sandra : Hello, Mike! What are you doing here?
　　　　嗨，麥克！你在這裏做什麼？

　Mike : I have an appointment with your boss.
　　　　我和妳的老闆有約。

Sandra : How is your family? 你家人好嗎？

　Mike : They are doing fine. Will I have to wait long?
　　　　他們很好。我會等很久嗎？

Sandra : No, my boss should be able to see you shortly.
　　　　不會，老闆很快就能見你。

SUBSTITUTION DRILLS /代換語句

1.

Hello, Mike !	What are you doing How come you are Why are you	here ?

➡ 嗨，麥克！你在這裏做什麽/你怎麽會在這裏？

2.

How's	your family ? your life going ? your business doing ?

➡ 你的家人/生活好嗎？
你的事業如何？

3.

No, my boss should be	able to see you with you	in a minute. shortly. very soon.

➡ 不，我的老闆很快就能見你。

4.

Could you	wait stay out	for a while ?

➡ 你能等/在外面等一會兒嗎？

** **How come ~** ? 〔話〕爲什麼～？

5.

You're looking	pretty smart today! great! good!

➡ 你今天看起來很好！

6.

It's been a while since	we last saw you. you visited us. you came around.

➡ 好久不見。

EXERCISE / 練習

◉模仿前面範例，完成下列對話。

Secretary : _____ , Daniel. What_____doing here？

  Visitor : I have an_____with your boss.

Secretary : How is your_____？

  Visitor : They are just fine. Will I_____long？

Secretary : No, my_____should be_____you shortly.

KEY TO EXERCISE / 解答

1. Hello, are you, appointment, family, have to wait, boss, able to see

2. Hi, can you be, important meeting, wife and children, be waiting, superior, with

UNIT 4　A Visitor Without an Appointment
未預約的訪客

SAMPLE DIALOGUE / 實況對話

Visitor : I'm here to see Mr. Baker. 我要見貝克先生。

Sandra : Do you have an appointment, sir ?
先生，你有事先預約嗎？

Visitor : I'm afraid not. Is there any way I could get
in his schedule on such short notice ?
恐怕沒有。雖然臨時才通知，可不可能請他挪出時間見我？

Sandra : Is it urgent ? 很緊急嗎？

Visitor : Yes, it's an urgent matter. 是的，是緊急事件。

Sandra : Alright. Let me just get Mr. Baker on the
line. 好，讓我用電話通知他。

** notice〔ˊnotɪs〕 *n.* 通知　　***on*（或 *at*）*short notice* 忽然；臨時

SUBSTITUTION DRILLS / 代換語句

1.

| Do you have an appointment ? |
| Are you scheduled to meet him today ? |

➡ 你有事先預約嗎？
你約定今天來見他嗎？

2.

I'm afraid, I have to	ask you to leave.
	send you away.
	tell you to come back again.

➡ 恐怕我必須請你離開／請你下次再來。

3.

I have to	check that first.
	refer to my appointment book.
	ask my boss.

➡ 我必須先查一下／查查我的紀錄／問老闆。

4.

| Please | follow | me. |
| | come with | |

➡ 請跟我來。

** *refer to* 查詢

5.

| I'll see | what can be done.
 what I can do.
 if he's busy. |

➡ 我會看看有沒有辦法。
我看看他忙不忙。

6.

| I do not | remember your calling me.
 recall your phone call. |

➡ 我不記得你會打電話來。

** recall〔rɪˈkɔl〕v. 想起

EXERCISE / 練習

◉ 模仿前面範例，完成下列對話。

Visitor : I＿＿＿＿＿ to see Mr. Stanley.

Secretary : ＿＿＿＿＿＿ , sir ?

Visitor : I'm afraid not. Is there any way I could get in his schedule ＿＿＿＿＿＿ ?

Secretary : Is it ＿＿＿＿＿ ?

Visitor : Yes, it's ＿＿＿＿＿ .

Secretary : Alright. Let me just get Mr. Stanley ＿＿＿＿＿＿ .

KEY TO EXERCISE / 解答

1. am here, Do you have an appointment, without an appointment, important, a pressing matter, for you

2. would like, Are you scheduled to meet him today, on such short notice, urgent, really urgent, on the line

---

A TIP FOR YOU / 秘書小點子

　　訪客進門時應該**立卽招呼**，若是正好在聽電話或與別人交談，應該先**點頭示意**，然後儘快結束手邊的事，專心招呼訪客。招呼訪客時要語氣誠懇，面帶笑容地說：
" Good morning, may I help you？"

　　遇到沒有事先預約的訪客，不要斷然回答上司在或不在，可先說 " *I'll see if he is available.* "（我看看他有沒有空。）然後向上司請示。若上司不願會見，要委婉地對訪客說上司不在或沒空，並請對方留下姓名與電話，表示再與之聯絡。

An Unexpected Visitor

意外的訪客

SAMPLE DIALOGUE / 實況對話

Sandra : Do you have an appointment, sir?
先生，你有事先預約嗎？

Visitor : No, I don't, I'm sorry. I'm Mr. Simpson,
Chairman of the Board. I just stopped by to
take a look around.
抱歉，沒有。我是董事長辛普森先生，我只是順道進來看看。

Sandra : I'll ring Mr. Baker —Mr. Baker, we have a
visitor. It's Mr. Simpson, Chairman of the Board.
我來叫貝克先生——貝克先生，我們有位訪客，董事長辛普森先生。

Mr. Baker: Oh God! What am I going to do? 天啊！怎麼辦？

Visitor : Relax, Mr. Baker, I'm not going to bite you.
別緊張，貝克先生，我不會把你吃了。

** ***stop by*** 順便拜訪　relax〔rɪ'læks〕 v. 放輕鬆　bite〔baɪt〕 v. 咬

SUBSTITUTION DRILLS ／代換語句

1. | Do you have
Did you make | an appointment ? |

　➡ 你有事先預約嗎？

2. | Mr. Baker, we have | a visitor.
a guest. |

　➡ 貝克先生，我們有位客人。

3. | But he | insists on seeing you.
demands to see you. |

　➡ 但是他堅持要見你。

4. | Your name doesn't | ring a bell.
sound familiar. |

　➡ 你的名字聽起來很陌生。

5. | Could you spell | your name
the word
your first name | again ? |

　➡ 你能把你的名字／那個字／你的姓再拼一遍嗎？

6.

Please	tone down your voice.
	don't get angry.
	don't make a scene here.

➡ 請降低你的音量／別生氣／不要在這裏大吵大鬧。

** *ring a bell* 激起回憶　　familiar〔fə'mɪljɚ〕*adj.* 熟悉的
tone down 降低　　　*make a scene* 大吵大鬧

EXERCISE ／練習 ▨▨▨▨▨▨▨▨▨▨▨▨▨▨

◉ 模仿前面範例，完成下列對話。

Secretary : _____an appointment？

Visitor : No, I don't,_____. I'm Mr. Bennett,
Chairman of the Board. I just stopped by
to take a look around.

Secretary : I'll ring Mr. Smith—Mr. Smith, we have a
_____. It's Mr. Bennett, Chairman of
the Board.

Boss : Oh my God！What_____？

Visitor : _____, Mr. Smith, I'm not going to
bite you.

KEY TO EXERCISE / 解答

1. Do you have, I'm sorry, visitor, am I going to do, Relax
2. Do you have, forgive me, guest, have I done, Take it easy

A TIP FOR YOU / 秘書小點子

　　有外賓來訪時，秘書可以口頭或親自帶領訪客至上司的辦公室。對於**第一次來訪**的訪客，秘書最好親自引見上司，這時可說，"*Mr. Baker, this is Mr. Green from A.B.C. Company.*" 若訪客爲**女性**，或者**地位或年齡高於上司**，則應將上司介紹給訪客，可說，"*Ms. Jackson, let me introduce Mr. Baker.*"

　　秘書爲訪客引見上司後，應向訪客**打聲招呼**後再離開，這時可說，"*May I be excused?*" 或者再加上一句，"*It was nice meeting you.*"

UNIT 6

Refusing a Visitor
拒絕訪客

SAMPLE DIALOGUE / 實況對話

Journalist : I am a journalist for the Sunday News, could your boss possible give me a few minutes?

　　　　　我是週日新聞的記者，妳的老闆能不能撥幾分鐘給我？

Sandra : I'm very sorry but he is booked the rest of this week, and he doesn't like to give interviews.

　　　　　很抱歉，他這個禮拜的時間全排滿了，而且他也不喜歡接受訪問。

Journalist : Can I arrange an appointment then?

　　　　　那麼我可以約個時間嗎？

Sandra : Leave me your card and I will call you back tomorrow. 請給我你的名片，我明天給你回電。

** journalist〔'dʒɜˋnlɪst〕 *n.* 新聞記者　book〔bʊk〕 *v.* 約定
interview〔'ɪntɚˏvju〕 *n.* 新聞記者的訪問

SUBSTITUTION DRILLS／代換語句

1.

I don't think my boss can	allow you much time. give you some time.

➡ 我想我的老闆可能不能見你。

2.

I'm sorry but	he is booked. his schedule is full. he is not available.

➡ 很抱歉，他的時間都排滿了。

3.

Please leave me	your card. your name and phone number. a brief message of your business.

➡ 請給我你的名片／名字和電話號碼。
　請大略告訴我你要找他談的事。

4.

Can't I just	make an appointment？ arrange a time to meet？

➡ 我能不能約個時間見面？

＊＊ available〔ə'veləbḷ〕*adj.* 有空的

5.

I will be happy to	tell the boss.
	pass along the message.
	give notice of your visit.

➡ 我很樂意代為轉達。

** *give notice of* 通知

EXERCISE / 練習

◉ 模仿前面範例，完成下列對話。

Visitor :　I'm a journalist for the Sunday News. May
I see your boss ?

Secretary :　I'm very sorry but he is＿＿＿and he
does not like to＿＿＿.

Visitor :　Can I＿＿＿an appointment then ?

Secretary :　Leave me your＿＿＿and I will＿＿＿.

KEY TO EXERCISE / 解答

1.　busy, give interviews, arrange, name and phone number, call
you back

2.　in a meeting now, entertain journalists, set, card, pass along
the message

UNIT 7 Maintenance People
維修人員

SAMPLE DIALOGUE / 實況對話

Maintenance : Excuse me, I'm here to fix the air conditioner. 對不起，我來修理冷氣機。

Sandra : Oh, it's down the hall on your left. Next
to the water fountain.
喔，沿著你左邊的走廊走。在噴泉旁。

Maintenance : What's the problem? 有什麼問題嗎？

Sandra : It's been smoking and making funny noises.
它會冒煙，還發出奇怪的聲音。

Maintenance : OK, I'll take a look at it. 好，我檢查看看。

Sandra : Let me know when you're finished.
修好的時候請告訴我。

** fix〔fɪks〕v. 修理　　*air conditioner* 冷氣機
fountain〔'faʊntn̩, -tɪn〕n. 噴泉

SUBSTITUTION DRILLS / 代換語句

1.

You must be here to	look at the air conditioner. repair the fax machine.

➡ 你一定是來檢查冷氣機的／修理傳真機的。

2.

The computer	has been acting strangely. hasn't been working properly. broke down the other day.

➡ 電腦的操作很奇怪／無法正常運作／幾天前故障了。

3.

It's down the hall	on your left. on your right. at the end.

➡ 那是在走廊的左邊／右邊／盡頭。

4.

Next to Opposite Above	the water fountain.

➡ 在噴泉旁／對面／上面。

** ***the other day*** 數天前　　opposite〔'ɑpəzɪt〕*prep*. 在～對面

5.

| It has been | making funny noises.
 buzzing and clicking. |

➡ 那部機器不斷發出奇怪的聲音。

6.

| Let me know
 Please tell me
 Report to me | when you're | finished.
 done. |

➡ 你修好時請告訴我。

EXERCISE / 練習

◉ 模仿前面範例，完成下列對話。

Maintenance : Excuse me, I'm here to fix the_____.

　Secretary : It's_____ on your left. Next to the_____.

Maintenance : What's the problem?

　Secretary : It's been smoking and making_____.

Maintenance : OK. I'll_____.

　Secretary : Let me know when you're_____.

KEY TO EXERCISE / 解答

1. air conditioner, down the hall, water fountain, funny noises, take a look at it, finished

2. coffee machine, downstairs, Manager's office, clicking sounds, check it out, done

Directing a Visitor

UNIT **8**

指引訪客

Please come in.

SAMPLE DIALOGUE / 實況對話

Delivery man : Excuse me, I have an order of lock sets to deliver. 對不起，我來送鎖。

Sandra : Oh, that would be a matter for the security department. 喔，請找安全部門。

Delivery man : Where would that be? 在哪裏呢？

Sandra : Go down the hall and turn left at the end of the hallway. The room is number 245. Just leave the order with the security guard at the desk.
沿著走廊走到盡頭之後左轉。房間號碼是二四五。
將鎖交給服務台的警衞就可以了。

＊＊ order〔'ɔrdə〕 *n.* 訂貨　hallway〔'hɔl,we〕 *n.* 走廊

SUBSTITUTION DRILLS / 代換語句

1.

Just leave the	merchandise boxes order	with the guard.

➡ 將這些貨品／盒子／訂貨交給警衛就行了。

2.

Let me just call the	personnel office. accounting office.

➡ 讓我打個電話給人事室／會計室。

3.

This	goes belongs	to the export department.

➡ 這屬於出口部。

4.

The girl over there should be able to	tell you. answer you. help you.

➡ 那邊那個女孩可以告訴／回答／幫助你。

** merchandise 〔'mɜtʃən,daɪz〕 n. 商品
  personnel 〔,pɜsn̩'ɛl〕 n. 人事部 export 〔'ɛksport〕 n. 出口

| 5. | Check with
Ask
Go see | the reception desk. |

➡ 請洽服務臺。

EXERCISE／練習

◉ 模仿前面範例，完成下列對話。

Delivery man : _____ me, I have _____ to deliver.

   Secretary : Oh, that would be a matter for the _____
                department.

Delivery man : Where would that be ?

   Secretary : Go down the hall and turn _____ at
                the end of the hallway. The room number
                is 245. Just leave the _____ with the
                _____ at the desk.

KEY TO EXERCISE／解答

1. Pardon, a package, accounting, right, package, clerk
2. Excuse, a box, administration, left, box, guard

UNIT 9　**Meeting Clients at the Airport**
接機

SAMPLE DIALOGUE ／實況對話 ≈≈≈≈≈≈

Sandra : I believe you are Mr. Taylor. 我想你是泰勒先生吧!
Mr. Taylor : Yes. 是的。

Sandra : Welcome to Taiwan. I'm Sandra, Mr. Baker's
secretary. He has asked me to come here
in his place to pick you up.

　　　　歡迎到台灣來。我是貝克先生的秘書珊德拉,他要我代
　　　　替他來這裏接你。

Mr. Taylor : Thank you. I have to get my luggage first.
謝謝。我必須先去領我的行李。

Sandra : Did you have a pleasant trip? 你的旅途愉快嗎?
Mr. Taylor : Yes, I did. 是的。

** *in* *one's* *place* 代替～　　*pick* *sb.* *up* 搭載～
luggage 〔'lʌgɪdʒ〕 *n.* 行李

SUBSTITUTION DRILLS / 代換語句

1.

| If I am not mistaken, I believe | you are Mr. Taylor. |

➡ 如果我沒弄錯的話，／我想你是泰勒先生吧。

2.

Welcome to Taiwan.
We're glad to have you here in Taiwan.
We've been anticipating your arrival.

➡ 歡迎到台灣來。
我們很高興你到台灣來。
我們一直期待你的到來。

3.

Did you have a pleasant trip?
Did you enjoy your trip?

➡ 你的旅途愉快嗎？

4.

| The | limousine car | is over here. |

➡ 轎車／車子在這裏。

** anticipate 〔æn'tɪsə,pet〕 v. 期待
limousine 〔'lɪmə,zin,,lɪmə'zin〕 n. 轎車

5.

> Can I carry that for you?
> Do you want me to help you with your bags?
> Please let me take some of your luggage.

➡ 要不要我幫你提那個／袋子？
　　請讓我幫你拿些行李。

EXERCISE／練習

● 模仿前面範例，完成下列對話。

Secretary：_____ you are Mr. Suzuki.

Mr. Suzuki：Yes.

Secretary：_____ Taiwan. I'm Jessica, Mr. Liu's secretary. He has asked me to come here _____ to pick you up.

Mr. Suzuki：Thank you. I have to get my luggage first.

Secretary：Did you _____ trip?

Mr. Suzuki：Yes, I did.

KEY TO EXERCISE／解答

1. If I am not mistaken, Welcome to, in his place, have a pleasant

2. I believe, We're glad to have you here in, in his absence, enjoy your

UNIT 16　Giving a Company Tour
帶領訪客參觀公司

SAMPLE DIALOGUE / 實況對話

Sandra : Welcome to our company. My name is Sandra, I'll be giving you a brief tour of our company today.

歡迎蒞臨本公司。我叫珊德拉,今天由我帶領各位參觀本公司。

Visitors : Is this your printing center ? 這是你們的印刷中心嗎?

Sandra : Yes. This section handles all of our printing needs. 是的。這一區負責所有的印刷事務。

Visitors : What happens in that section over there ?

那邊那個區域呢?

Sandra : That is where we ship our products.

那是我們運送產品的地方。

** section 〔'sɛkʃən〕 *n*. 區域　handle〔'hændl〕 *v*. 處理
ship〔ʃɪp〕 *v*. 運送

SUBSTITUTION DRILLS/代換語句 ▨▨▨▨▨▨▨▨▨▨▨▨▨▨▨▨

1.

Welcome to our Glad to have you visit our We're happy you could come see our	company.

➡ 歡迎蒞臨本公司。

2.

I will give you a	brief quick little	tour.

➡ 我將帶你們大略地參觀。

3.

We have	over 100 many quite a few	employees.

➡ 我們有一百多位/很多/相當多員工。

4.

This is where we	ship assemble build	our products.

➡ 這是我們運送/裝配/製造產品的地方。

** *quite a few* 相當多　　employee〔͵ɛmplɔɪˊi〕*n.* 員工
assemble〔əˊsɛmbḷ〕*v.* 裝配

5.

This is	the accounting department. the employees' lounge area. where we keep our files.

➡ 這是會計部／員工交誼廳／存放檔案的地方。

＊＊ lounge〔laʊndʒ〕 *n.* 休息室

EXERCISE ╱ 練習 ▨▨▨▨▨

◉ 模仿前面範例，完成下列對話。

Secretary : Welcome to our＿＿＿＿＿. I will＿＿＿＿＿.

  Visitors : How large is your company ?

Secretary : We have＿＿＿＿＿ employees.

  Visitors : Is this your＿＿＿＿＿ center ?

Secretary : Yes. This＿＿＿＿＿ handles＿＿＿＿＿ of our
printing needs.

  Visitors : What happens in that section over there ?

Secretary : That is where＿＿＿＿＿ our products.

KEY TO EXERCISE /解答

1. company, give you a brief tour, over 100, printing, section, most, we build

2. company, show you our operation, many, main, part, a lot, we assemble

---

A TIP FOR YOU /秘書小點子

秘書代替上司前往機場迎接客戶前，應先掌握客戶的外形特徵，以節省找人的時間。在機場與客戶初次見面，要**先表明自己的身份**，" *I'm Sandra, Mr. Baker's secretary.* "或" *I'm Sandra Lin of Drexler Corporation.* " 若有同事隨行，則應一併做簡單介紹。

UNIT 11 Entertaining a Guest
招待客人

SAMPLE DIALOGUE / 實況對話

Sandra : Let's break for lunch now. 現在我們休息吃中飯吧！

Guest : That's a good idea. Never talk business on an empty stomach. 好主意。空著肚子不談生意。

Sandra : Do you prefer Chinese or Western food?
你喜歡中式食物還是西式食物？

Guest : Either one is OK with me. 都可以。

Sandra : I know of a nice Mongolian Barbeque near here.
我知道這附近有一家蒙古烤肉不錯。

Guest : That sounds great! I've never eaten Mongolian food before. 聽起來不錯！我從來沒有吃過蒙古烤肉。

** Mongolian 〔mɑŋˋgolɪən〕 *adj*. 蒙古的
barbeque 〔ˋbɑrbɪ͵kju〕 *n*. 烤肉

SUBSTITUTION DRILLS / 代換語句

1.

Let's	break for lunch take a lunch break go to lunch	now.

➡ 現在我們休息吃中飯吧！

2.

Never talk business Never make a decision	on an empty stomach.

➡ 空著肚子不談生意／不做決定。

3.

Do you prefer Which do you prefer, Would you rather have	Chinese or Western food?

➡ 你喜歡中式食物還是西式食物？

4.

I know of a There is a	nice	Mongolian Barbeque Japanese restaurant	near here.

➡ 我知道這附近有一家蒙古烤肉／日本料理不錯。

5.

Is there anything that	you can't eat? you are not allowed to eat? you can't have?

➡ 有沒有什麼東西你不能吃？

6.

| I'm sure you'll | like love enjoy | what I've ordered. |

➡ 我相信你會喜歡我點的菜。

EXERCISE／練習

◉ 模仿前面範例，完成下列對話。

Secretary : Let's_____lunch now.

Guest : That's a good idea. Never_____on an
empty stomach.

Secretary : _____Chinese or Western food？

Guest : _____.

Secretary : I know of a nice Mongolian Barbeque_____.

Guest : _____! I've never eaten Mongolian food
before.

KEY TO EXERCISE／解答

1. break for, talk business, Do you prefer, Either one's OK with
me, near here, That sounds great

2. go to, make a decision, Would you like, Up to you, in the area,
Wonderful

UNIT **12** **Sightseeing**
觀光遊覽

SAMPLE DIALOGUE / 實況對話

Sandra : Would you like to go sightseeing tomorrow?
　　　　 你明天想不想四處遊覽？

Client : Not a bad idea! 這主意不錯！

Sandra : What would you like to see in Taipei?
　　　　 你想看看台北的哪些地方？

Client : Well, let's see. I'd like to go to Snake Alley,
　　　　 the Shihlin Night Market and the Chiang Kai-
　　　　 shek Memorial Hall.

　　　　 嗯，我想想。我想去華西街、士林夜市和中正紀念堂。

Sandra : I'll pick you up here tomorrow. 明天我來這裏接你。

＊＊ sightseeing〔'saɪt,siɪŋ〕n. 遊覽；觀光
　　 memorial〔mə'morɪəl,-'mɔr-〕adj. 紀念的

SUBSTITUTION DRILLS / 代換語句

1.

Would you like to	go sightseeing see the sights tour the city	tomorrow?

➡ 你明天想不想四處遊覽？

2.

What would you like to see Where would you like to go	in Taipei?

➡ 你想參觀台北哪些地方？

3.

I can	pick you up see you meet you	at your hotel.

➡ 我可以去飯店接你。

4.

We can go to	the Shihlin Night Market. Snake Alley. Chiang Kai-shek Memorial Hall.

➡ 我們可以去士林夜市／華西街／中正紀念堂。

** sights〔saɪts〕 n. pl. 名勝

5.

| We can take | a break
some time off
a day off | tomorrow. |

➡ 我們明天可以休息一下／一天。

6.

| I'm sure you'll | like it.
find it nice.
never forget it. |

➡ 我相信你一定會喜歡／覺得很好／終生難忘。

EXERCISE /練習

◉模仿前面範例，完成下列對話。

Secretary : Would you like to＿＿＿＿＿tomorrow?

Client : ＿＿＿＿＿!

Secretary : ＿＿＿＿＿in Taipei ?

Client : Well, let's see. I'd like to＿＿＿＿Snake
Alley, the Shihlin Night Market and Chiang
Kai-shek Memorial Hall.

Secretary : I'll＿＿＿＿here tomorrow.

KEY TO EXERCISE ╱解答

1. go sightseeing, Not a bad idea, What would you like to see, visit, see you

2. tour the city, Good idea, Where would you like to go, go to, pick you up

---

A TIP FOR YOU ╱秘書小點子

帶領客戶觀光遊覽**應事先做好計劃**。除了詢問客戶意見，安排好路線，還要注意天候狀況，途中並需安排休憩用餐的地方。觀光時秘書須充當嚮導，**爲客戶做簡介**，因此平時最好多充實名勝古蹟的背景知識，使客戶留下深刻印象。

行程表範例

ITINERARY FOR MR. M. BAKER
Oct. 2—4

October 2 (Wed.)

　10 : 00　Lv. Taipei (CX 604)

　12 : 56　Ar. Narita Airport, Tokyo

　13 : 30　Check in at the Ambassador Hotel

　15 : 00　Meeting with Mr. Suzuki of the
　　　　　AA Company at the hotel

October 3 (Thu.)

　10 : 00　Staff meeting at Tokyo Branch
　　　　　Office

　13 : 30　The party of the AA Company at
　　　　　the hotel

　18 : 00　Dinner with Mr. Green of the AZ
　　　　　Inc.

October 4 (Fri.)

　a.m.　　Free

　13 : 00　Lv. Tokyo (CX 604)

　15 : 56　Ar. Taipei

　＊Note: Hotel address and phone numbers
　　　　　are in attached sheet.

CHAPTER 3

Interoffice
Communications

與同事聯繫

Schedule ○○○

UNIT 1 Calling About Appointments
打電話提醒約會

SAMPLE DIALOGUE / 實況對話

Sandra： Mr. Clay? 克雷先生嗎？

Mr. Clay： Yes, it is. 是的，我就是。

Sandra： I just want to remind you of your meeting with Mr. Baker tomorrow morning.
我只是要提醒你明天早上和貝克先生有約。

Mr. Clay： Thanks for reminding me, Sandra.
謝謝妳提醒我，珊德拉。

Sandra： I'll see you tomorrow then. 那麼明天見。

Mr. Clay： Yes. Bye. 好，再見。

** *remind* sb. *of* sth. 提醒某人～

SUBSTITUTION DRILLS／代換語句

1.

I'm calling	for Mr. Baker. about your appointment with Mr. Baker.

➡ 我替貝克先生打電話。
我打電話提醒你和貝克先生有約。

2.

You have	an appointment a meeting a scheduled lunch	with Mr. Baker tomorrow.

➡ 你和貝克先生約定明天見面／一起吃午餐。

3.

Thanks for	reminding me. calling. the call.

➡ 謝謝你提醒我／打電話來。

4.

Be sure Don't forget Remember	to bring the file.

➡ 記得帶檔案來。

| 5. | See you
I'll be expecting you
I'll be meeting you | tomorrow. |

➡ 明天見。

EXERCISE / 練習

◉模仿前面範例，完成下列對話。

> *Secretary* : _____?
>
> *Mr. Foley* : _____.
>
> *Secretary* : I just want to remind you of your_____
> with Mr. Hazlitt tomorrow morning.
>
> *Mr. Foley* : Thanks for_____me, Lydia.
>
> *Secretary* : I'll_____you tomorrow then.
>
> *Mr. Foley* : _____. Bye.

KEY TO EXERCISE / 解答

1. Mr. Foley, Yes it is, appointment, reminding, meet, Yes

2. May I have Mr. Foley, Speaking, scheduled lunch, telling, see, That's right

UNIT 2 **Distributing Materials**
分送資料

SAMPLE DIALOGUE / 實況對話 ▨▨▨▨▨▨▨▨▨▨▨

Sandra : Is Mr. Morgan in？莫根先生在嗎？

Miss Blake : He's not in yet. Can I do anything for
you？他還沒來，妳有什麼事嗎？

Sandra : Well, I have some brochures I'd like to
give to him. 嗯，我有些小冊子要給他。

Miss Blake : Why don't you just leave them with me
and I'll give it to him as soon as he arrives. 妳可以交給我，等他一來我就給他。

Sandra : Thanks. Do you know where I can find Miss
Dawson？ I have to give these letters to her.
謝謝。妳知道道生小姐在哪裏嗎？我必須把這些信件交給她。

** brochure〔bro'ʃʊr〕*n.* 小冊子

SUBSTITUTION DRILLS / 代換語句

1.

Is Mr. Morgan	in ? around ? here, yet ?

➡ 莫根先生在嗎？

2.

I have some	brochures mail	to give to him.

➡ 我有些小冊子 / 信件要交給他。

3.

Can I	leave them with you ? entrust you with them ? ask you to give it to him ?

➡ 我能請你轉交嗎？

4.

Do you know where	Sarah Mr. Drake the new recruit	is ?

➡ 你知道莎拉 / 杜雷克先生 / 新進人員在哪裏嗎？

** entrust〔ɪnˈtrʌst〕v. 委託　　recruit〔rɪˈkrut〕n. 新成員

5.

I still have to	find Mr. Holmes. distribute these memos.

➡ 我還要找霍姆茲先生／分送這些信函。

6.

Mr. Baker	asked me to give this to him. sent me here to distribute these copies.

➡ 貝克先生要我把這個交給他／叫我來發這些影印資料。

** distribute〔dɪ'strɪbjʊt〕v. 分送

EXERCISE ／練習

◉ 模仿前面範例，完成下列對話。

Secretary : Is Mr. Norris＿＿＿＿？

Miss Cruise : He hasn't ＿＿＿＿ in yet. Can I do
　　　　　　　＿＿＿＿ for you?

Secretary : Well, I have some＿＿＿＿I'd like to
　　　　　　give to him.

Miss Cruise : Why don't you just leave them with me
　　　　　　and I'll＿＿＿＿it to him as soon as
　　　　　　he arrives.

Secretary: Thanks. Do you know where I can ＿＿＿＿＿

Miss Quincy ? I have to ＿＿＿＿ these

letters to her.

KEY TO EXERCISE /解答

1. around , punched , something , letters , give , find , distribute

2. in , reported , anything , materials , give , find , deliver

---

━A TIP FOR YOU /秘書小點子━

秘書每天都要處理許多信件，學習有效的信件處理法，
可省下不少時間與麻煩。秘書在過濾信件時，要注意信
內所提的**附件**（ *enclosure* ）是否齊全，以及信上有無**日
期**與**回信地址**；若無回信地址，則應將信封與信函、信
件一起附上，無日期則標上郵戳（ *post mark* ）日期。
信件過濾分類後，再分送給上司、公司其他相關人員，
或留下來自己處理。

UNIT 3　Requests for Information
詢問消息

In Mr. Stone's office.

Thank you.

SAMPLE DIALOGUE / 實況對話 ▓▓▓▓▓▓▓▓▓▓

Sandra : Ms. Burns, where can I find the results
of the Carlsten account?
　　　柏恩斯小姐，哪裏可以查到卡爾斯頓帳目的結算？

Ms. Burns : In Mr. Stone's office. 在史東先生的辦公室。

Sandra : Can you ask him to draw up a summary?
　　　妳能不能請他寫份摘要？

Ms. Burns : He has already written the final report.
He'll send it to Mr. Baker in the morning.
　　　他已經寫好完整的報告了，今天早上會送去給貝克先生。

Sandra : Thank you. 謝謝。

** account 〔 əˋkaʊnt 〕 *n.* 帳目　　***draw up* 草擬**
summary 〔 ˋsʌmərɪ 〕 *n.* 摘要

SUBSTITUTION DRILLS / 代換語句 ▨▨▨▨▨▨▨▨▨

1.

Where	can I find are	the results of the	ABC meeting? Troy account?

➡ 哪裏可以查到ABC會議的結果 / 特洛伊帳目的結算？

2.

He just finished	closing the deal. talking over the case. discussing the account.

➡ 他剛接到訂單 / 談完這筆生意 / 討論完這份帳目。

3.

Can you tell him to	write up draw up	a closing report? a summary?

➡ 你能不能請他寫份完整的報告 / 摘要？

4.

Mr. Baker would like to see	the outcome. the results.

➡ 貝克先生想要知道結果。

** deal〔dɪl〕n. 交易　outcome〔'aʊt,kʌm〕n. 結果

5.

| Can you | fill me in on
answer
help me with | some questions that
I have ? |

➡ 你能回答我一些問題嗎？

6.

| Are you | busy right now ?
doing anything at the moment ?
free to help me out ? |

➡ 你現在忙 / 有事要做 / 能幫我的忙嗎？

EXERCISE /練習

● 模仿前面範例，完成下列對話。

Secretary : Ms. Porter, where are the results of the

　　　　　　　_____ ?

Ms. Porter : In Mr. Scott's office. He just finished

　　　　　　　_____ .

Secretary : Can you ask him to_____ a summary ?

　　　　　　　Mr. Green would like to see the_____ .

Ms. Porter : He has already written_____ . He'll

　　　　　　　send it to Mr. Green in the morning.

Secretary : _____ .

KEY TO EXERCISE /解答

1. ABC meeting, closing the deal, draw up, results, his conclusions, Thank you
2. Troy account, discussing the account, write, outcome, the final report, That'll be all for now

---

A TIP FOR YOU /秘書小點子

所有的約會來臨之前，秘書都應打電話**再確定**（*recon-firm*）**一次**。若知道上司開會時間延長，可能影響隨後的約會，應打電話至會議地點，請示上司是否變更約會時間。若上司與高級主管如董事長或總經理開會，則可打電話給高級主管的秘書解釋情況，請求轉達。

UNIT 4 Requests for Help
請求幫忙

SAMPLE DIALOGUE / 實況對話

Sandra : Mr. Mosley? Mr. Baker doesn't understand some of the budget graphs. Is there any way you could help him?

莫斯利先生嗎？貝克先生有些預算表不懂。你能不能幫幫忙？

Mr. Mosley : Alright. Tell him to be in my office in 45 minutes. 好。告訴他四十五分鐘後來我辦公室。

Sandra : Should I instruct him to bring his copy of the report? 我必須請他帶預算報告的影印本嗎？

Mr. Mosley : No, that's not necessary. 不必。

** budget〔'bʌdʒɪt〕*n.* 預算　　graph〔græf , grɑf〕*n.* 圖表

SUBSTITUTION DRILLS／代換語句

1.

| Mr. Baker | doesn't understand
can't make out | some of the
budget graphs. |

➡ 貝克先生有些預算表不懂。

2.

| Sorry for | interrupting.
the interruption.
disturbing you. |

➡ 抱歉打擾你。

3.

| I'll try to | call
page
reach | Mr. Hansen for help. |

➡ 我會試著請韓森先生幫忙。

4.

| If he | is not able to
can't
is unable to | help, can I call you
instead? |

➡ 如果他不能幫忙，我可以找你嗎？

** make out 理解　　instead〔ɪnˊstɛd〕*adv*. 代替

5.

| Can you | look at this
solve this
check this out | for me ? |

➡ 你能不能幫我看看 / 解決 / 檢查這個？

EXERCISE /練習

◉ 模仿前面範例，完成下列對話。

Secretary : Mr. Hopkins_____ some of the budget graphs.

Mr. Irving : I'll be very happy to help him, but it will have to wait for half an hour. I am in a _____ right now.

Secretary : Sorry for_____. Would later on be fine?

Mr. Irving : Yes,_____. Send him to my office in 45 minutes.

Secretary : Should I_____ him to bring his copy of the report?

Mr. Irving : That's alright. I have a copy here.

KEY TO EXERCISE /解答

1. can't understand, conference, disturbing you, it'd be fine, ask

2. can't make out, meeting, the interruption, it would be OK, tell

UNIT 5 Introductions

介紹

SAMPLE DIALOGUE / 實況對話

Sandra: Who's our new office mate?
誰是我們的新工作伙伴?

Mr. Baker: Sandra, I'd like you to meet Becca, Becca Gritz. She will be working with you starting today.
珊德拉,介紹妳認識貝卡,貝卡·葛莉斯。
從今天開始,她將和妳一起工作。

Sandra: Welcome to Drexler Corporation, Becca! We're really happy to have you.
貝卡,歡迎加入德瑞斯勒公司!眞高興妳成爲我們的一員。

Becca: Thank you. I'm glad to be here.
謝謝。我很高興能來。

** mate〔met〕n. 伙伴

SUBSTITUTION DRILLS / 代換語句

1.

Who's our new	office mate ? member ? addition ?

➡ 誰是我們的新工作伙伴 / 新成員 ?

2.

I'd like to introduce This is I'd like you to meet	Ms. Becca Gritz.

➡ 介紹你認識貝卡・葛莉斯小姐 。

3.

Welcome.   Glad to have you here.   I hope you'll like it here.

➡ 歡迎 。
　　很高興你來 。
　　希望你喜歡這裏 。

4.

If you've got any problems you can	ask come to	me.

➡ 如果你有任何問題 ，可以來找我 。

** addition〔ə'dɪʃən〕n. 增加物

5.

| I hope we can | work well together.
be good friends.
help one another. |

➡ 我希望我們能合作愉快／成爲好朋友／互相幫忙。

6.

| Please | feel at home.
call me Sandra.
feel free to ask me anything. |

➡ 請別拘束。
　請直呼我珊德拉。
　有事請儘管問我。

EXERCISE /練習 ▨▨▨▨▨▨▨▨▨▨▨▨▨▨▨▨▨▨▨▨

◉ 模仿前面範例，完成下列對話。

Secretary : Who's＿＿＿＿＿?

　　Boss : Chris, I'd like＿＿＿＿＿Betty, Betty
　　　　　　Jackson.

Secretary : Welcome to Drexel, Betty！ We're really
　　　　　　happy＿＿＿＿＿.

New-comer : Thank you. I'm＿＿＿＿＿.

KEY TO EXERCISE / 解答

1. our new office mate , you to meet , to have you , glad to be here

2. the new face , to introduce , you chose to work here , looking forward to my job here

---

A TIP FOR YOU / 秘書小點子

與人見面**握手**（ *shake hands* ）寒喧是基本的禮節，以下是握手一般的原則。

㈠**同性**之間，一般是由**年紀長或職位高的一方**先伸手。不過男士們握手寒喧已經成為一種習慣，因此常常是雙方同時伸手；至於女士們是否握手則依各人喜好而定。

㈡**異性**之間，通常是由**女士**選擇是否握手。但如果男士先伸出手來，女士也必須伸手，否則就太使對方難堪了。

UNIT 6 Having Lunch
吃午餐

SAMPLE DIALOGUE／實況對話

Jean: Sandra, it's time for lunch. 珊德拉，吃午飯了！

Sandra: Let me just put away these things. Could you go on ahead without me? I bought some lunch today. 讓我把這些東西收拾一下。妳能不能自己去？我今天已經買了午餐。

Jean: Are you sure? We're eating at that Cantonese Restaurant over by the corner.
妳確定嗎？我們要到轉角那家廣東餐廳吃。

Sandra: I'm sure, could you just buy some fruits on your way back? Some pears or apples would be nice.
我確定。妳能不能回來時順便買點水果？幾個梨或蘋果都好。

** **put away** 存放　　Cantonese〔͵kæntən'iz〕*adj.* 廣東的

SUBSTITUTION DRILLS／代換語句

1.

It's time	for lunch. to eat. to take a break.

➡ 吃午飯了／吃飯了／休息了。

2.

Let me just	put away these things. finish this. clear my desk.

➡ 等我把這些東西收拾一下／等我把這個做完／等我整理好桌子。

3.

Could you	go on ahead have lunch eat	without me?

➡ 你能不能自己去／吃午餐／吃？

4.

I'm	sure. trying to save some money. on a diet.

➡ 我確定／想省錢／在節食。

** *on a diet* 照規定飲食；在節食

5.

Could you just buy some fruits	on your way back? for me? after eating?

➡ 你能不能回來時 / 爲我 / 吃完後買點水果？

EXERCISE／練習

● 模仿前面範例，完成下列對話。

  Dora：Sylvia, it's time＿＿＿＿＿.

Secretary：Let me just＿＿＿＿＿. Could you go on

    ＿＿＿＿＿. I＿＿＿＿＿some lunch today.

  Dora：Are you＿＿＿＿＿?.

Secretary：I'm＿＿＿＿＿. Could you just buy some

    fruits＿＿＿＿＿?

KEY TO EXERCISE／解答

1. to eat, clear my desk, without me, prepared, sure, on a diet,
   on your way back

2. for lunch, finish this, ahead without me, bought, certain, sure,
   after your lunch

UNIT 7 Delegating Responsibilities
分配任務

SAMPLE DIALOGUE / 實況對話

Sandra : Rose, is this you？是羅絲嗎？

Rose : Yes, what's up？是的，有什麼事？

Sandra : This is Sandra. Would you mind taking charge of decorating the office for our Christmas party？
我是珊德拉，妳願不願意負責將辦公室佈置成耶誕晚會的會場？

Rose : Sure. 當然願意。

Sandra : You can get your supplies upstairs from Mrs. Horn. 妳可以到樓上霍恩太太那兒拿需要的東西。

Rose : Will I be getting any help？有沒有人可以幫我的忙？

Sandra : You can ask Frank and Cathy to help you.
妳可以找法蘭克和凱西幫忙。

** ***take charge of*** 承辦　　decorate〔ˈdɛkəˌret〕*v.* 裝飾

SUBSTITUTION DRILLS／代換語句

1.
Is this Rose ?
Rose, is that you ?
Rose ?

➡ 是羅絲嗎？

2.
I have a	load of things million things lot	to do.

➡ 我有一大堆事情要做。

3.

You can	get your supplies from Mrs. Horn.
	buy whatever you need and charge it
	  to the company.
	request for some materials from the
	  Administration Department.

➡ 你可以從霍恩太太那兒拿到需要的東西／買你需要的東西再
向公司報帳／向行政部門申請所需的東西。

4.
You can ask Frank and Cathy to	help you. give you a hand.

➡ 你可以找法蘭克和凱西幫忙。

5.

| Would you mind | taking charge of the party?
decorating the mess hall?
being in charge of the Xmas party? |

➡ 你願意負責宴會 / 裝飾餐廳 / 負責耶誕晚會嗎？

** ***mess hall*** （工廠、軍隊等的）餐廳
　　Xmas〔ˈkrɪsməs〕*n.* 耶誕節（= *Christmas* ）

EXERCISE / 練習

◉ 模仿前面範例，完成下列對話。

Secretary : _____ ?
　　Rose : Yes, _____ ?

Secretary : This is Judith. Would you mind _____ ?
　　Rose : Sure.

Secretary : You can get your _____ from Mrs. Horn.
　　Rose : Will I be getting any _____ ?

Secretary : You can ask Frank and Cathy to _____ .

KEY TO EXERCISE / 解答

1. Rose , what's up , decorating the mess hall for the party ,
   materials , assistance , help you

2. Is this Rose , what can I do for you , taking charge of the
   party , supplies , help , give you a hand

UNIT 8 Editing Copy
修改原稿請人重打

SAMPLE DIALOGUE / 實況對話

Sandra : Phyllis, can you re-type this for me?
　　　　菲莉絲，妳能不能幫我重打這份？

Phyllis : Alright. When do you want it?
　　　　好的。妳什麼時候要？

Sandra : As soon as possible. This is urgent.
　　　　愈快愈好，這很急。

Phyllis : Will there be anything else?
　　　　還有別的事要交待嗎？

Sandra : Just be careful with the spelling.
　　　　請小心拼字。

** urgent〔'ɝdʒənt〕adj. 急迫的

SUBSTITUTION DRILLS／代換語句

1.

Can you	re-type re-do re-work	this for me?

➡ 你能不能替我重打／重做這個？

2.

This is	urgent. rush. important.

➡ 這很緊急／重要。

3.

We have a	guideline for this. form to follow. standard to stick to.

➡ 我們有個方針／格式／標準要遵守。

4.

Be careful with the	spelling. indentations. change of typeface.

➡ 小心拼字／每段開頭要空字／要換字體。

** rush〔rʌʃ〕*adj.* 緊急的　　guideline〔'gaɪd,laɪn〕*n.* 指導方針
stick to 堅守　　indentation〔,ɪndɛn'teʃən〕*n.*（每段首行的）縮格
typeface〔'taɪp,fes〕*n.* 鉛字的字體

5.
> Type this in a letterhead.
> Use the memo form.
> Put the manuscript in a folder.

➡ 用公司的信紙打 。
用便箋的形式 。
將原稿放入檔案夾中 。

＊＊ manuscript〔′mænjə,skrɪpt〕n. 原稿

EXERCISE / 練習

◉ 模仿前面範例，完成下列對話 。

Secretary : Can you＿＿＿＿this for me ?
　　　Typist : Alright.＿＿＿＿do you want it ?

Secretary : ＿＿＿＿. This is＿＿＿＿.
　　　Typist : Will there be anything else ?

Secretary : Just be careful with the＿＿＿＿.

KEY TO EXERCISE / 解答

1. re-work , How soon , As soon as possible , urgent , spelling

2. re-type , When , By tomorrow , rush , indentations

CHAPTER 4

Telephone Calls

以電話應對

UNIT 1　The Boss Is in and Free to Talk
上司有空聽電話

SAMPLE DIALOGUE / 實況對話

（phone rings）（電話響）

Sandra : Drexler, may I help you?
德瑞斯勒公司。我能為你效勞嗎?

Caller : Yes, I'd like to speak to Mr. Baker.
我想請貝克先生聽電話。

Sandra : May I ask who's calling? 請問哪位?

Caller : This is Mr. Stewart, his accountant.
我是他的會計師史圖爾特先生。

Sandra : Please hold. I'll see if he's in. (To Mr. Baker) Sir, Mr. Stewart is on the phone. Do you wish to talk to him?
請稍等,我看他在不在。(對貝克先生說)先生,史圖爾特先生找你。你要跟他說話嗎?

Mr. Baker : Yes, of course. Put him through. 當然,請接進來。

SUBSTITUTION DRILLS / 代換語句

1.

Drexler,	may I help you? can I help you? how can I help you?

➡ 德瑞斯勒公司。我能為你效勞嗎?

2.

Mr. Baker	has been waiting for has been expecting	your call.

➡ 貝克先生一直在等你的電話。

3.

May I ask who's calling? Who's calling, please? To whom am I speaking, please?

➡ 請問哪位?

4.

Please hold.	I'll see if he's in. I'll tell him you're calling.

➡ 請稍等,我看他在不在 / 我告訴他你打電話來。

5.

Do you wish	to talk to him? to speak with him?

➡ 你要跟他說話嗎?

6.

Mr. Stewart	is on the phone. is calling. is on Line 1.

➡ 史圖爾特先生打電話來 / 在一線。

EXERCISE / 練習

◉ 模仿前面範例，完成下列對話。

Secretary: Taiwan Plastics, _____?

    Caller: Yes, I'd like to talk to Mr. Dell.

Secretary: May I ask who's_____?

    Caller: This is_____,_____.

Secretary: _____. I'll see if he's_____.

(To Boss): Sir, _____is on the line. Do you wish
to talk to her / him?

    Boss: Yes, of course._____.

KEY TO EXERCISE / 解答

1. may I help you, on the line, Mrs. Dell, his wife, Just a
   second, around, your wife, Put her through

2. can I help you, calling, Greg, his lawyer, Wait a minute,
   available, Greg, Put him through

UNIT 2　The Boss Is Not in the Office
上司不在辦公室

At the moment, he is out of the office.

SAMPLE DIALOGUE /實況對話

Sandra：Hello, Drexler. 喂，德瑞斯勒公司。

Mr. Lewis：Hello, this is Mr. Morrison Lewis. I'd like to speak to Mr. Baker, please.
我是莫利森·路易斯先生。請貝克先生聽電話。

Sandra：Just a moment. (pause) I'm sorry, at the moment he's out of the office. Would you like to leave your number?
稍等。(停頓)抱歉，他現在不在辦公室。你要留電話嗎?

Mr. Lewis：Please have him call me at my office. He knows the number.
請他打電話到我辦公室。他知道號碼。

Sandra：Of course. 好。

SUBSTITUTION DRILLS /代換語句

1.

Hello, Good Afternoon, Good Morning,	Drexler.

➡ 喂／午安／早安，德瑞斯勒公司。

2.

May I ask who	is calling? is on the line? am I speaking to?

➡ 請問哪位？

3.

At the moment, he's	out of the office. in a meeting. busy.

➡ 他現在不在辦公室／正在開會／很忙。

4.

Just a moment. Hold, please. Hold on a minute.	I'm sorry, at the moment he's out of the office.

➡ 請稍等。很抱歉，他現在不在辦公室。

5.

Would you like to leave	your number?
	your name?
	your company's name?

➡ 你要留電話號碼 / 名字 / 公司名稱嗎？

EXERCISE / 練習

◉ 模仿前面範例，完成下列對話。

Secretary : Hello, IDM.

　　Voice : ＿＿＿＿＿, this is Carl Stevens. I'd like
　　　　　　to＿＿＿＿＿Mr. Lear, please.

Secretary : Just a moment. I'm sorry, at the moment
　　　　　　he's＿＿＿＿＿. Would you like to leave
　　　　　　your number?

　　Voice : Please have him＿＿＿＿＿at my＿＿＿＿＿.
　　　　　　He knows the number.

Secretary : Yes, good-bye.

KEY TO EXERCISE / 解答

1. Hello, speak with, in a meeting, contact me, home
2. Good afternoon, talk to, out for lunch, call me, office

UNIT 3　Taking a Message

受理留言

SAMPLE DIALOGUE / 實況對話

Sandra : Hello, Drexler. 喂，德瑞斯勒公司。

Voice : I'd like to speak to Michael Baker, please.
我想請麥可‧貝克聽電話。

Sandra : I'm sorry, Mr. Baker is not in. May I take a message? 很抱歉，貝克先生不在。你要留言嗎？

Voice : Yes. Tell him Mr. Cook called and ask him to return my call as soon as he gets back.
好的。告訴他庫克先生找他，並且請他儘快回電。

Sandra : Alright, Mr. Cook. I'll have Mr. Baker call you back as soon as he gets here.
好的，庫克先生。他一回來我就請他回電。

SUBSTITUTION DRILLS / 代換語句

1.

| Can I have
Can you get me | Mr. Baker, please? |

➡ 請找貝克先生聽電話。

2.

| Mr. Baker is not in | at the moment.
right now.
at present. |

➡ 貝克先生目前不在。

3.

| May I take
Would you like to leave
Do you have | a message? |

➡ 你要留言嗎？

4.

| I'll be sure he | gets
gets hold of
receives | the message. |

➡ 我一定會轉告他。

5. | Would you like him | to call you back? |
   | | to return your call? |

➡ 你要他回電嗎?

EXERCISE / 練習 ▓▓▓▓▓▓▓▓▓▓▓▓▓▓▓▓▓▓▓

◉模仿前面範例,完成下列對話。

Secretary : Hello, Oriental.

    Voice : I'd like to speak to Mr. Victor Clark, please.

Secretary : I'm sorry, Mr. Clark _____. _____?

    Voice : Yes. Tell him Mr. Dryden called and ask him to _____ as soon as he _____.

Secretary : Alright, Mr. Dryden. I'll have Mr. Clark _____ as soon as possible.

KEY TO EXERCISE / 解答 ▓▓▓▓▓▓▓▓▓▓▓▓▓▓▓▓▓

1. is not in right now, Can I take a message, return my call, can, call you back

2. is in a meeting at the moment, Would you like to leave a message, come to my office, is available, see you

UNIT 4　Transferring Calls
轉接電話

SAMPLE DIALOGUE / 實況對話 ▨▨▨▨▨▨▨▨▨▨▨▨

Caller : May I have Peter, please? 請找彼得。

Sandra : Which Peter do you want? We have two
　　　　 Peters in the office.
　　　　　你找哪一位彼得？我們辦公室裏有兩位彼得。

Caller : I believe it's Mr. Peter Sun. 應該是孫彼得先生。

Sandra : This is Mr. Baker's office but I'll transfer
　　　　 your call to Mr. Sun's office anyway. Don't
　　　　 hang up.
　　　　　這裏是貝克先生的辦公室，但是我會幫你把電話接到孫先生
　　　　　的辦公室。別掛斷。

Caller : Thank you very much. 眞謝謝妳。

　** transfer〔træns'fɝ〕*v.* 移轉　　***hang up*** 掛斷電話

SUBSTITUTION DRILLS / 代換語句 ▨▨▨▨▨▨▨▨▨▨▨▨▨▨

1.

| We have | no Peter
two Peters | here. |

➡ 我們這裏沒有／有二個彼得。

2.

| Don't | hang up.
put down your phone.
drop the line. |

➡ 別掛斷。

3.

| This is Mr. Baker's office.
This is not Mr. Sun's office.
Mr. Sun has his own phone. |

➡ 這裏是貝克先生的辦公室。
這裏不是孫先生的辦公室。
孫先生有他的專線。

4.

| Can I ask | what number you are calling?
who you are calling?
who do you want? |

➡ 請問你打幾號／找誰？

5.

The operator patched you into the wrong	line. extension. connection.

➡ 接線生接錯了。

6.

Could you	call dial phone	again ?

➡ 你能不能再撥一次？

** patch〔pætʃ〕v. 連接電路　extension〔ɪkˈstɛnʃən〕n. 內線電話

EXERCISE / 練習

◉ 模仿前面範例，完成下列對話。

Caller : May I _____ Philip, please ?

Secretary : Which Philip do you want ?　We have _____ in the office.

Caller : _____ it's Mr. Philip Chen.

Secretary : This is _____ office but I'll transfer your call to Mr. Chen's office, anyway. Don't _____.

Caller : Thank you very much.

KEY TO EXERCISE / 解答

1. talk to , a Philip Chen and a Philip Wang , I believe , Mr. Cole's , hang up

2. have , two Philips , If I am not mistaken , not his , drop the line

---

A TIP FOR YOU / 秘書小點子

遇到必須將電話轉到其他部門的情況時，要以親切的語調將原因告訴對方（例如由其他部門承辦，上司不在請別人代為處理等），並**將電話轉到適當部門**，避免讓對方覺得受敷衍而感到不愉快。

UNIT 5　Calling for the Boss
替上司打電話

SAMPLE DIALOGUE / 實況對話

Mr. Smith : This is Mr. Smith on the phone.
　　　　　　　我是史密斯先生。

Sandra : Mr. Smith, it seems that the ship carry-
　　　　　　ing your merchandise was blown off course
　　　　　　by a typhoon.
　　　　　　史密斯先生，運載你貨物的船好像被颱風吹離了航道。

Mr. Smith : In that case, there's not much we can do,
　　　　　　　is there? 如果是那樣的話，我們也沒辦法，不是嗎？

Sandra : We're sorry for the delay. 我們很抱歉延期交貨。

Mr. Smith : Don't worry. These things happen.
　　　　　　　別擔心。這些事是常有的。

** course〔kors, kɔrs〕*n.* 航道　　delay〔dɪ'le〕*n.* 延期

SUBSTITUTION DRILLS / 代換語句

1.

Mr. Baker has asked me	to talk to you. to give you a call. to call you.

➡ 貝克先生要我打電話給你 。

2.

The ship	was blown off course. sank on the high seas. collided with another ship.

➡ 船被吹離航道 / 在外海沈沒 / 和另一艘船相撞 。

3.

We	are sorry for the loss. regret the loss.

➡ 我們為這次的損失感到抱歉 。

4.

You will be compensated	justly. adequately. properly.

➡ 你會得到適當的賠償 。

** ***high seas*** 外海 collide〔kə'laɪd〕 *v.* 相撞
compensate〔'kɑmpən,set〕 *v.* 賠償

5.

| This is beyond | our control. |
| | our reach. |

➡ 這不是我們能控制的。
　　這超出我們能力所及。

** *beyond one's reach* 能力所不能及

EXERCISE / 練習

◉ 模仿前面範例，完成下列對話。

Voice : This is Mr. Smith.

Secretary : Mr. Smith, it_____that the ship
　　　　　_____your_____was blown off
　　　　　course by a_____.

Voice : In that case, there's_____we can do,
　　　　is there?

Secretary : We're sorry for the_____.

Voice : Don't_____. These things happen.

KEY TO EXERCISE / 解答

1. seems, carrying, merchandise, typhoon, nothing, loss, worry

2. appears, transporting, goods, hurricane, not much, delay,
   think about it

UNIT 6 **Making Appointments**

定約會

SAMPLE DIALOGUE ／實況對話

Sandra : Mr. Baker would like to set up an appointment with you. Will you be available tomorrow morning ?

貝克先生想和你約個時間見面。明天早上你有空嗎？

Mr. Eliot : Tomorrow morning will be fine. What time
can he come over ?

明天早上可以。他什麼時候過來？

Sandra : Will 10 a.m. be convenient ? 上午十點鐘方便嗎？

Mr. Eliot : I'll put his name on the 10 a.m. slot.

我會把他的名字記在十點的位置。

** convenient〔kən'vinjənt〕*adj.* 方便的　　slot〔slɑt〕*n.* 位置

SUBSTITUTION DRILLS / 代換語句

1.

Mr. Baker would like to	arrange set up fix	an appointment with you.

➡ 貝克先生想和你約個時間見面。

2.

Will you be available tomorrow? Will tomorrow be alright with you? Can we set the appointment tomorrow?

➡ 明天早上你有空嗎?

3.

Will 10 a.m. be convenient? Will you have time at about 10 a.m.? He would like to meet you at around 10 a.m.

➡ 你早上十點方便 / 有空嗎?
他希望在十點左右見你。

4.

I'll call you again tomorrow to	confirm it. make sure. verify it.

➡ 我明天會再打電話確定。

** verify〔ˈvɛrəˌfaɪ〕*v.* 確認

5.

| He will be free | all morning.
tomorrow.
the whole day on Saturday. |

➡ 他整個早上 / 明天 / 星期六整天都有空。

6.

I'll mention it to him.
I'll tell him about it.

➡ 我會告訴他。

** mention〔'mɛnʃən〕*v*. 提及

EXERCISE / 練習

◉ 模仿前面範例，完成下列對話。

　　Secretary : Mr. Forster would like to＿＿＿＿an
　　　　　　　　 appointment with you. Will＿＿＿＿?

Mr. Fletcher : Tomorrow morning will be＿＿＿＿.
　　　　　　　　What time can he come over?

　　Secretary : Will＿＿＿＿?

Mr. Fletcher : I'll put his name on the 10 a.m.
　　　　　　　　＿＿＿＿.

KEY TO EXERCISE / 解答

1. fix , tomorrow morning be alright , fine , 10 a.m. be convenient , slot

2. set up , you be available tomorrow morning , fine , you have time at about 10 a.m. , slot

A TIP FOR YOU / 秘書小點子

秘書常有機會代表上司與客戶約定會面時間。要注意的是，預約後必須**經過上司確認**，若上司認爲不妥，應立即通知對方更改或取消，因此預約時務必留下**預約者的連絡電話**，以防萬一。

UNIT 7 Changing Appointments
變更約會時間

SAMPLE DIALOGUE / 實況對話

Sandra : Mrs. Thatcher? Mr. Baker asked me to tell you that he won't be able to make it tomorrow morning.

佘契爾女士嗎？貝克先生要我告訴妳，他明天早上無法赴約。

Mrs. Thatcher : Is there anything wrong? 出了什麼事嗎？

Sandra : Well, he'll tell you about it himself on Friday morning. Will you be free by then?

呃，他星期五早上會親自告訴妳。妳那個時候有空嗎？

Mrs. Thatcher : Friday morning is fine with me.

星期五早上可以。

SUBSTITUTION DRILLS /代換語句 ▨▨▨▨▨▨▨▨

1.

This is	Sandra, Mr. Baker's secretary.
	Mr. Baker's secretary, Sandra.
	Sandra, from Mr. Baker's office.

➡ 我是貝克先生的秘書珊德拉。

2.

I'm sorry I think	he won't be available by then.

➡ 很抱歉，他那時沒空。

3.

Mr. Baker	asked me instructed me told me	to call you.

➡ 貝克先生要我打電話給你。

4.

He'll	tell explain it to apologize to	you himself.

➡ 他會親自告訴你 / 向你解釋 / 向你道歉。

** apologize〔ə'pɑlə,dʒaɪz〕v. 道歉

5.

He won't be able to make	it. it for your appointment.

➡ 他無法赴約。

6.

Will you be	free available ready	by then?

➡ 你那個時候有空嗎？

EXERCISE / 練習

●模仿前面範例，完成下列對話。

Secretary: Mrs. Thomas, this is _____ .

Mrs. Thomas: Hello, Maria. Are you calling about
_____ ?

Secretary: In fact yes, Mr. Swift _____ me to
tell you that he won't be able to _____
tomorrow morning.

Mrs. Thomas: Is there anything _____ ?

Secretary: Well, he'll _____ you himself on Friday morning. Will you _____ by then?

Mrs. Thomas: Friday morning _____ .

KEY TO EXERCISE / 解答

1. Mr. Swift's office , my appointment , wants , make it , wrong , explain it to , be free , will be fine
2. Mr. Swift's secretary , tomorrow , asked , come , the matter , tell , be available , suits me fine

---

A TIP FOR YOU / 秘書小點子

　　秘書應該確切掌握上司的行蹤，以便有重要訪客或電話時可以聯絡上。

　　有電話找上司而上司不在時，無論對方是否要求留話，禮貌上秘書都應該主動詢問"*Do you like to leave a message*?" 或 "*May I take a message*?" 如果對方願意留話，秘書必須**正確地**將留話內容記錄下來，並最好**重述一次**，以確定無誤。若對方表示希望上司回電，別忘了要他留下電話號碼。

UNIT 8 Overseas Calls
國際電話

I would like to make a long distance call.

SAMPLE DIALOGUE / 實況對話

Operator: Overseas operator, may I help you?
國際台接線生,我能為你服務嗎?

Sandra: Yes, I would like to make a long distance call to New York. 是的,我要打一通長途電話到紐約。

Operator: May I have the number? 請告訴我電話號碼。

Sandra: The area code is 304, and the number is 384-3948. 區域號碼三○四,電話號碼是三八四三九四八。

Operator: Will it be collect or charged to Taipei?
是對方付費還是台北方面付費?

Sandra: Collect. 對方付費。

Operator: One moment, please. 請稍等。

** *area code* 區域號碼　　collect〔kə'lɛkt〕*adj.* 由對方付費的

SUBSTITUTION DRILLS / 代換語句

1.

I would like to make	a long distance an overseas	call.

➡ 我要打一通長途 / 國際電話。

2.

It'll be a	person-to-person station-to-station credit card	call.

➡ 這是一通叫人 / 叫號 / 記帳電話。

3.

Charge it to	Taipei. New York. this number.

➡ 請由台北 / 紐約 / 這個電話號碼付費。

4.

One moment, Just a second, Hold on,	please.

➡ 請等一下。

5.

Could you	try call dial	again ?

➡ 你能不能再撥一次？

6.

What's the	area code for Los Angeles ? country code for Bermuda ?

➡ 洛杉磯的區域號碼是多少？
百慕達的國碼是多少？

EXERCISE / 練習

◉ 模仿前面範例，完成下列對話。

Operator : Overseas operator, may I help you ?

Secretary : Yes, I would like to make＿＿＿＿call to
the States.

Operator : May I have the number ?

Secretary : The number is＿＿＿＿.

Operator : Will it be＿＿＿＿or＿＿＿＿?

Secretary : ＿＿＿＿.

Operator : ＿＿＿＿, please.

KEY TO EXERCISE /解答

1. an overseas, 234-2349, area code 123, charged to Taipei, New York, Taipei, Hold on

2. a long distance, (043) 348-2934, person-to-person, station-to-station, Person-to-person, Just a minute

★ A TIP FOR YOU /秘書小點子

目前打國際電話可以不透過接線生而直撥（稱爲**國際直撥電話**，*International Direct Dialing*）。撥號時必須先撥當地**國際冠碼**，再撥對方**國碼、區域號碼**，最後撥**電話號碼**。例如：由台灣（國際冠碼 002）打到法國（國碼 33）尼斯（區域號碼 93）的 781-4266，必須撥 002-33-93-7814266。

但如果要打**叫人電話**（ person-to-person call），**對方付費電話**（ collect call）或是**記帳電話**（ credit card call），就必須透過接線生（ operator）來轉接。方法是先撥給國際台，對接線生說明通話種類，如果是叫人電話，還得報出受話人姓名，最後說明對方的區域號碼與電話號碼。另外還有一種**叫號電話**（station-to-station call），適合在不指定跟某人通話時使用。至於**國際會議電話**（*conference call*），是三個人以上同時透過國際電話，進行會議的方式，十分便利。

UNIT 9 A Call from the Boss' Wife
上司夫人來電話

SAMPLE DIALOGUE／實況對話

Mrs. Baker : Hello, Sandra. Could you tell Mr. Baker that his wife is calling?

嗨，珊德拉。請告訴貝克先生他太太找他。

Sandra : I wish I could, Mrs. Baker, but he just stepped out.

但願我能，貝克太太，但是他剛才出去了。

Mrs. Baker : Is he coming back soon? 他很快就會回來嗎？

Sandra : He should be returning in a couple of minutes. Can I have him call you?

他幾分鐘後應該會回來。要請他回電嗎？

Mrs. Baker : No thanks, I'll call back later.

不用了，謝謝。我等會兒再打。

SUBSTITUTION DRILLS／代換語句

1.

| I wish
If only | I could, Mrs. Baker. |

➡ 但願我能，貝克太太。

2.

| He just | stepped out.
left the office.
went out. |

➡ 他剛出去。

3.

| He should be returning in | a couple of
several
a few | minutes. |

➡ 他幾分鐘後應該會回來。

4.

| Do you want | to leave a message?
the number at the plant? |

➡ 你要留言／工廠的電話嗎？

** plant〔plænt〕 n. 工廠

5.

Can I have him	call you?
	return your call?
	call you back?

➡ 要請他回電嗎？

EXERCISE / 練習

◉ 模仿前面範例，完成下列對話。

Boss' wife : Hello, Rita, could you tell Mr. Browning
                that_____is calling?

Secretary : _____I could, Mrs. Browning, but he
              just_____.

Boss' wife : _____soon?

Secretary : He should be returning in_____minutes.
              Can I have him_____?

Boss' wife : No, thanks, I'll_____later.

KEY TO EXERCISE / 解答

1. his wife , I wish , stepped out , Is he coming back , a couple of ,
   call you , call back

2. Mrs. Browning , If only , left the office , Will he be coming
   back , several , return your call , try

UNIT 16 **Wrong Number**
打錯電話

SAMPLE DIALOGUE / 實況對話

Caller : Hello, is this the ACME Bermuda Shorts Company？喂，請問是頂好短褲公司嗎？

Sandra : No, I'm sorry. You have gotten a wrong number. 很抱歉，不是，你打錯了。

Caller : Is this 931-7070？這是九三一七〇七〇嗎？

Sandra : That's our number but this is Drexler Corporation. Perhaps you should call the operator.
那是我們的號碼，但是這裏是德瑞斯勒公司。或許你可以問問接線生。

Caller : This is an excellent idea. Thank you for your patience. 好主意。謝謝妳這麼有耐心。

Sandra : It was no trouble at all. 沒什麼。

** *Bermuda shorts* 百慕達式短褲　　patience〔'peʃəns〕*n.* 耐心

SUBSTITUTION DRILLS / 代換語句

1.
No,	I'm sorry. it isn't. I'm afraid not.

➡ 很抱歉，不是。

2.
You have	gotten reached	a wrong number.

➡ 你打錯了。

3.
That's	our our company's the right	number.

➡ 那是我們 / 我們公司 / 正確的號碼。

4.
It was	no trouble nothing	at all.

➡ 沒什麼。

5.
They have	changed given us	their number since 6 months ago.

➡ 他們六個月前已經換號碼了 / 把他們的號碼給我們了。

EXERCISE / 練習

◉ 模仿前面範例,完成下列對話。

Caller: Hello, is this the ABC Furniture Company?

Secretary: No,_____. You have_____a wrong number.

Caller: Is this 931-7070?

Secretary: That's_____number but this is Road-runner Manufacturing._____you should call the operator.

Caller: That is_____idea. Thank you for your _____.

Secretary: It was_____at all.

KEY TO EXERCISE / 解答

1. I'm sorry, gotten, our, Perhaps, an excellent, patience, no trouble

2. it isn't, reached, our company's, Maybe, a great, time, nothing

UNIT 11　Tour Arrangements
安排旅行

SAMPLE DIALOGUE / 實況對話 ▨▨▨▨▨▨▨▨▨▨▨▨▨▨▨

Sandra : My boss would like to join your packaged tour
of Malaysia. Are there still any tickets left?

　　　　我的上司想參加你們馬來西亞的包辦旅行團，你們還有名
　　　　額嗎？

Phoenix : You called just in time. We still have a few
tickets left.

　　　　妳電話打的正是時候，我們還有一些名額。

Sandra : Alright, thank you very much. I'll call you
back to confirm the reservation.

　　　　好，非常謝謝你。我會再打給你，確定預約。

＊＊ *package(d) tour* 包辦旅行（交通、膳宿均由旅行社負責的旅行）
　　confirm〔kən'fɝm〕*v.* 確定

SUBSTITUTION DRILLS／代換語句

1.

My boss would like to	join go with take part in	the packaged tour of Malaysia.

➡ 我的上司想參加馬來西亞的包辦旅行團。

2.

Is there still room for one more? Are there any tickets left? Are there any slots left?

➡ 還有名額嗎？

3.

Is there any way he can stay longer? Does he have to join all the activities? Can he bring along a Malaysian friend of his?

➡ 他有沒有辦法待久一點？
　　所有活動他都必須參加嗎？
　　他能不能帶一位馬來西亞的朋友同行？

4.

I have to	ask confirm it with check with	my boss.

➡ 我必須問問我的上司。

5.

I need to know	the departure date.
	the customs regulations there.
	what the weather there will be like.

➡ 我必須知道出發時間 / 當地海關的規定 / 當地的氣候 。

** departure〔dɪ'pɑrtʃɚ〕*n.* 出發　　customs〔'kʌstəmz〕*n.* 海關

EXERCISE／練習

◉ 模仿前面範例，完成下列對話 。

Secretary : My boss would like to_____your_____
　　　　　　 tour of Malaysia. Are there any_____
　　　　　　 left？

　　Agent : You called just_____time. We still
　　　　　　 have a few tickets left.

Secretary : Alright, thank you very much. I'll call you
　　　　　　 back to_____the reservation.

KEY TO EXERCISE／解答

1. join , guided , vacancies , at the right , make
2. take part in , group , tickets , in , confirm

A Hotel Reservation
訂旅館

SAMPLE DIALOGUE / 實況對話

Hotel Worker: Asiaworld Hotel, how can I help you?
環亞飯店，我能為你效勞嗎？

Sandra: I'd like to book a room from August 21st to 25th for a Mr. Michael Baker.
我想為一位麥可・貝克先生訂房間，從八月二十一日到二十五日。

Hotel Worker: Would you like a single or a double room?
要單人房還是雙人房？

Sandra: Please reserve the Presidential Suite.
請幫我保留總統套房。

** reserve〔rɪˈzɝv〕*v.* 保留；預訂
presidential〔ˌprɛzəˈdɛnʃəl〕*adj.* 總統的　suite〔swit〕*n.* 套房

SUBSTITUTION DRILLS / 代換語句

1.

| I'd like to | book a room
reserve a room
make a room reservation | from August 21st to 25th. |

➡ 我想預訂一個房間，從八月二十一日到二十五日。

2.

| I would like | a single.
a room facing the pool.
a regular room. |

➡ 我要一個單人房 / 面對游泳池的房間 / 普通的房間。

3.

| Please reserve | the Presidential Suite.
a suite.
two adjoining rooms with double beds. |

➡ 請保留總統套房 / 一間套房 / 兩間相鄰的雙人房。

4.

| Charge it to
Debit
Put it on | the account of Drexler Corporation. |

➡ 將費用記入德瑞斯勒公司的帳中。

** adjoining〔əˈdʒɔɪnɪŋ〕*adj.* 相鄰的　debit〔ˈdɛbɪt〕*v.* 記入～帳中

5.

He will	be arriving be checking in	on August 21st.

➡ 他八月二十一日會住進去。

** *check in* （到旅館登記）住宿

EXERCISE / 練習

◉ 模仿前面範例，完成下列對話。

Hotel Worker: Asiaworld Hotel. May I help you?

　Secretary: _____ to_____ a room from
　　　　　　　 August 21st to 25th for a Mr. Donald
　　　　　　　 Trump.

Hotel Worker: Would you_____ a single or a double
　　　　　　　 room?

　Secretary: Please reserve_____.

Hotel Worker: OK. that will_____ 84,300 NT
　　　　　　　 dollars. How_____?

　Secretary: You may_____ the account of New
　　　　　　　 Asia Company, Inc.

KEY TO EXERCISE / 解答 ▨▨▨▨▨▨▨▨▨▨▨▨▨▨▨▨▨▨▨▨▨▨▨▨▨▨▨

1. I'd like , book , like , the Presidential Suite , total , will you be paying , charge it to

2. I want , reserve , prefer , your finest suite , be , do you wish to pay , put it on

---

A TIP FOR YOU / 秘書小點子

秘書在為上司預訂旅館時，應說明所需房間的種類。一般旅館房間有下列幾種：(1)**單人房，單人床**（ single room, single bed ）(2)**單人房，雙人床**（ single room, double bed ）(3)**雙人房，雙人床**（double room, double bed ）(4)**雙人房，二張單人床**（ double room, *twin beds* ）(5)**套房**（ suite ）(6)**連接房**—兩房間有門相通（ connecting room ）(7)**鄰接房**—兩房間相鄰（adjoining room ）。另外，房間浴室有with/without bath（有／無浴室）以及with shower（只有淋浴設備）的區別，應一併指明。

UNIT 13 A Plane Reservation
訂機票

SAMPLE DIALOGUE / 實況對話

Sandra : Phoenix Travel Agency？是鳳凰旅行社嗎？

Phoenix : Yes. This is Phoenix Travel Agency. May I help you？的,這是鳳凰旅行社。需要我效勞嗎？

Sandra : This is Drexler Corporation. I would like to book a flight to Paris on January 8 on Air France, First Class and round trip.
這裏是德瑞斯勒公司。我要訂一張前往巴黎的來回票,一月八號,法航,頭等艙。

Phoenix : Under whose name shall I write the ticket？機票上要寫哪一位的名字？

Sandra : Mr. Baker, Michael Baker. 麥可・貝克先生。

** phoenix〔'finɪks〕 *n.* 鳳凰　　agency〔'edʒənsɪ〕 *n.* 代理商
round trip 來回旅行

SUBSTITUTION DRILLS / 代換語句

1.

| I would like to | book a flight
buy a ticket
reserve a seat | to Paris. |

➡ 我要訂一個前往巴黎的機位。

2.

| He would like to fly
He'll be leaving | on January 8. |

| Is there any available flight on January 8 ? |

➡ 他預定一月八號啓程。
一月八號有沒有班機?

3.

| Please make that | First Class.
Business Class.
Economy Class. |

➡ 請給我頭等艙 / 商務艙 / 經濟艙。

4.

| Make it | an open-end ticket.
a round-trip ticket.
a one-way ticket. |

➡ 給我無限期的票 / 來回票 / 單程票。

** open-end〔'opən'εnd〕 adj. 無限制的

5.	Address the ticket Write it Make it	to Mr. Michael Baker.

➡ 機票上寫麥可・貝克先生。

EXERCISE / 練習 ▨▨▨▨▨▨▨▨▨▨▨▨▨▨▨▨▨▨

◉模仿前面範例，完成下列對話。

    Secretary：＿＿＿＿＿？

Travel Agency：Yes. May I＿＿＿＿you？

    Secretary：This is Pacific Corporation. I would
              like to＿＿＿＿to Paris on January 8
              on＿＿＿＿, ＿＿＿＿and＿＿＿＿.

Travel Agency：Under whose name shall I＿＿＿＿the
              ticket？

    Secretary：Mr. Wilson, John Wilson.

KEY TO EXERCISE / 解答 ▨▨▨▨▨▨▨▨▨▨▨▨▨▨▨▨

1. Evergreen Travel Agency , do anything for , book a flight , any
   airline , Business Class , round trip , address

2. Is this Evergreen , help , reserve a seat , China Airlines ,
   Economy Class , single journey , write

UNIT **14** **A Restaurant Reservation**

訂餐廳座位

SAMPLE DIALOGUE / 實況對話

Sandra : I would like to reserve a table for a party of four.

我想預訂一張四人的桌位。

Restaurant : Will that be for lunch or dinner?

是午餐還是晚餐?

Sandra : It'll be for lunch. Reserve it under the name of Mr. Baker. They should be there at around 12:15.

午餐,以貝克先生的名義。他們在十二點十五分左右會抵達。

Restaurant : 12:15 it is. 十二點十五分,好的。

SUBSTITUTION DRILLS / 代換語句

1.

I would like to reserve	a table. a function room. a hall.

➡ 我想預訂一個桌位 / 一個房間 / 一個廳 。

2.

We will be There will be We will have	five in the party.

➡ 我們總共有五位 。

3.

Do you serve	breakfast? dessert? coffee?

➡ 你們有沒有供應早餐 / 點心 / 咖啡 ?

4.

Reserve it under the name of Mr. Baker. Mr. Baker will head the party. Mr. Baker will be hosting the lunch.

➡ 請以貝克先生的名義訂位 。
　 貝克先生是這個餐會的主人 。

** *function room* 餐館中隔開的房間 　 host〔host〕*v.* 作東

5.
| Can we order ahead of time?
| Can we use a credit card to pay the bill?
| What do you recommend for lunch?

➡ 我們可不可以事先訂餐／以信用卡付帳？
午餐你推薦什麼菜？

** recommend 〔,rɛkə'mɛnd〕v. 推薦

EXERCISE ∕ 練習 ══════════════

◉ 模仿前面範例，完成下列對話。

Secretary: I would like to reserve a＿＿＿＿＿for a
party of four.

Restaurant: Will＿＿＿＿＿be for lunch or dinner?

Secretary: It'll be for lunch. Mr. Baker will＿＿＿＿.
They should＿＿＿＿at around 12:15.

Restaurant: 12:15 it＿＿＿＿.

KEY TO EXERCISE ∕ 解答 ══════════════

1. function room , that , be hosting the lunch , arrive , will be

2. table , the reservation , head the party , be there , is

UNIT 15 Giving the Company Address
給公司地址

Could you give me your company's address?

SAMPLE DIALOGUE／實況對話

Sandra : Drexler, may I help you?

　　　　德瑞斯勒公司，我能為你效勞嗎？

Mr. Brown : Hello. This is Mr. Brown speaking. Sandra, could you give me your company's address again?

　　　　喂，我是布朗先生。珊德拉，妳能不能再告訴我一次貴公司的地址。

Sandra : Alright, Mr. Brown. We're on Fuhsing North Road, number 36, seventh floor. We're right at the corner of Minchuan East Road and Fuhsing North Road. Will that do?

　　　　好的，布朗先生。我們這裏是復興北路三十六號七樓，就在民權東路與復興北路的轉角處。這樣清楚嗎？

Mr. Brown : That's OK. Thanks a lot. 清楚，謝謝。

SUBSTITUTION DRILLS / 代換語句

1. | Drexler, may I help you?
Hello. This is Drexler Corporation.
Good morning. Drexler Corporation. |

➡ 德瑞斯勒公司，我能為你效勞嗎？
   喂 / 早安，這裏是德瑞斯勒公司。

2. | We're on
You can find us at
Our address is | Fuhsing North Road, number 36, seventh floor. |

➡ 我們的地址是復興北路三十六號七樓。

3. | We're right | at the corner of Minchuan East Road and Fuhsing N. Rd.
across the Cathay Plaza.
between Minchuan East Road and Minsheng East Road. |

➡ 我們在民權東路與復興北路的轉角處 / 國泰廣場對面 /
   民權東路和民生東路之間。

** plaza 〔ˈplæzə, ˈplɑzə〕 n. 廣場

4.

Will that	do? be O.K. ? be alright ?

➡ 這樣可以嗎？

5.

Call me if you still can't find	the address. our place. our company.

➡ 如果你還是找不到，再打電話給我。

6.

You're welcome. Don't mention it. The pleasure is mine.

➡ 不客氣。

EXERCISE /練習

◉ 模仿前面範例，完成下列對話。

Secretary: Unix Corporation, may I help you?

Caller: _____. This is Mr. Hwang of 3 Coils
Corporation. _____ Mr. Barton today.
I've lost your address. _____me where
your company is ?

Secretary: _____, Mr. Hwang,_____Fuhsing
North Road, #36, 7 F. We're right_____
Minchuan and Fuhsing. Will that_____?

Caller: That's fine. Thanks a lot.

KEY TO EXERCISE / 解答 〰〰〰〰〰〰〰〰〰〰

1. Yes, I have an appointment with , Could you tell , Sure , we're on , at the corner of , do

2. Hello , I'm supposed to meet , Do you mind telling , Alright , you can find us at , between , be OK

┌──*A TIP FOR YOU* /秘書小點子〰〰〰〰┐

在英文書信中，地址的寫法是**由小到大**，與中文相反。
例如：2 F., 43 Roosevelt Road, Sec. 2,
Taipei, Taiwan 10021
R.O.C.
然而在**口語**中，也可以依中文的習慣來說，如上面的地
址也可以讀作：Roosevelt Road Section Two Number Forty-Three Second Floor.

└────────────────────────┘

UNIT 16　Calling for Repairs
請人修理

SAMPLE DIALOGUE / 實況對話

Sandra : Hello, is this Mark? 喂，是馬克嗎？

Mark : Hello Sandra. What can I do for you today?
嗨，珊德拉。今天有需要我效勞的地方嗎？

Sandra : My printer has broken down again.
我的印表機又壞了。

Mark : What happened? 怎麼了？

Sandra : The paper just won't go in. Can you come
over and take a look at it?
紙送不進去。你能不能過來看看？

Mark : I'll be there right away. 我馬上來。

Sandra : Thanks, Mark. I knew I could count on you.
謝謝，馬克。我就知道可以找你幫忙。

SUBSTITUTION DRILLS / 代換語句

1.

Is this	Mark?
	the service department?
	IDM Computers?

➡ 是馬克 / 服務部 / IDM電腦公司嗎?

2.

My printer	has broken down	again.
	is acting up	

➡ 我的印表機又壞了。

3.

I knew	I could count on you.
	I could depend on you.
	you wouldn't disappoint me.

➡ 我就知道可以找你幫忙 / 你不會讓我失望。

4.

Can you	come over?
	take a look at it?
	see what's wrong with it?

➡ 你能不能來看看出了什麼毛病?

** printer〔'prɪntɚ〕*n.* 印表機　　*count on* 依賴
act up 出毛病　　disappoint〔͵dɪsə'pɔɪnt〕*v.* 使失望

5. | The paper just won't go in.
    The machine just eats up the paper.
    The printer just crumples the paper.

> ➡ 紙送不進去。
> 機器會吃紙。
> 印表機會把紙弄皺。

** crumple〔'krʌmpḷ〕 v. 弄皺；壓皺

EXERCISE / 練習

◉ 模仿前面範例，完成下列對話。

Secretary : Hello, is this Mark?

　　Mark : Hello, _____ . What _____ today?

Secretary : My printer _____ again.

　　Mark : What _____ ?

Secretary : The printer just _____ .
　　　　　　　 Can you _____ ?

　　Mark : I'll be there _____ .

Secretary : Thanks, Mark. I knew _____ .

KEY TO EXERCISE / 解答

1. Miss Li, can I do for you, broke down, is wrong, eats up the paper, come over, right away, I could count on you

2. Nora, is it, is at it, happened, won't go in, take a look at it, as soon as I can, you wouldn't fail me

---

A TIP FOR YOU / 秘書小點子

秘書在打電話前,最好用小紙條**擬好備忘錄**,寫上對方的電話號碼、姓名與職務,並將**要告訴對方的事項**列出,以免有所遺漏。此外,若是要找的人不在,是要留話(leave a message)、待會兒再打還是請對方撥過來,最好一併寫上。至於談話內容或結果,也可以寫在備忘錄的空白處,非常方便。

UNIT 17 Canvassing
問價

> Is that your best price?

SAMPLE DIALOGUE / 實況對話

Sandra: How much would a ream of bond paper cost?
一令銅版紙要多少錢？

Supplier: Are you ordering in bulk or in small quantities? 妳要買多或少？

Sandra: Well, we need 50 reams. 呃，我們需要五十令。

Supplier: The price is NT$ 50 per ream.
價錢是每令五十元台幣。

Sandra: Is that your best price? 這是你們的最低價嗎？

Supplier: Not unless you can buy more. 除非妳買更多。

Sandra: Alright, I'll call you back. 好，我會再給你電話。

** ream〔rim〕*n.* 令（紙張單位，480 張或 500 張）
bond paper 銅版紙　　*in bulk* 大量地

SUBSTITUTION DRILLS /代換語句

1.

How much would	a ream of bond paper cost ?
	you charge me for a ream of bond paper ?
	I have to pay for a ream of bond paper ?

➡ 一令銅版紙多少錢？

2.

| Well, | I've been asked to buy we need | 50 reams. |

➡ 呃，我要買／我們需要五十令。

3.

We'd like to give you	the order.
	the business.
	the contract.

➡ 我們很想給你們訂單。

4.

| We've been | old loyal consistent | customers of yours. |

➡ 我們是你們的老主顧。

5.

Is that	your best price ?
	the best you can do ?

➡ 這是你們的最低價嗎？

6.

We saw your name in the directory.
You were recommended.
We saw your billboard around the corner.

➡ 我們在電話簿上看到你們的名字。
有人推薦你們。
我們在轉角處看到你們的廣告。

** directory〔dəˈrɛktərɪ, daɪ-〕 n. 電話簿
recommend〔ˌrɛkəˈmɛnd〕 v. 推薦
billboard〔ˈbɪlˌbord〕 n. 廣告招貼板

EXERCISE / 練習

◉ 模仿前面範例，完成下列對話。

Secretary : How much would_____?
  Supplier : Are you_____in bulk or in small
          quantities ?

Secretary : Well,_____50 reams.
  Supplier : The price is NT$50 per ream.

Secretary : Is that_____?

  Supplier : Not_____you can buy more.

Secretary : Alright, I'll call you_____.

KEY TO EXERCISE / 解答

1. you charge me for a ream of bond paper , ordering , we need , your best price , if , again

2. I have to pay for a ream of bond paper , buying , I've been asked to buy , the best you can do , unless , back

---

A TIP FOR YOU / 秘書小點子

▶ 辦公室設備的名稱 ◀

bulletin board（佈告欄）	coffee pot（咖啡壺）
computer（電腦）	fax（傳眞機）
file tray（文件用淺盤）	filing cabinet（檔案櫃）
intercom（對講機）	iron safe（保險櫃）
paper shredder（碎紙機）	photocopier（影印機）
potted plant（盆栽）	slide projector（幻燈片放映機）
telex（商務電報交換機）	time clock（打卡鐘）
typewriter（打字機）	water dispenser（飲水機）
white board（白黑板）	word processor（文書處理機）

UNIT 18　Purchasing Office Supplies
購買辦公用品

SAMPLE DIALOGUE／實況對話

Vogue : Vogue Furniture. 時尚家具行。

Sandra : This is Drexler Corporation. I would like to order 2 office-style cabinets. We want them in white. The catalogue number is 90-F-2356.

這裏是德瑞斯勒公司。我要訂購兩個辦公櫃，白色的。目錄編號是九〇－F－二三五六。

Vogue : How soon do you want it? 妳要多快送到？

Sandra : Could you deliver it here by tomorrow afternoon? 你能不能明天下午以前送到？

** vogue〔vog〕*n.* 時尚

corporation〔͵kɔrpə'reʃən〕*n.* 股份有限公司

cabinet〔'kæbənɪt〕*n.* 櫃　　catalogue〔'kætḷ͵ɔg〕*n.* 目錄

SUBSTITUTION DRILLS / 代換語句

1.

I would like to order 2	office-style of your cheapest	cabinets.

➡ 我想訂購二個辦公櫃 / 最便宜的櫃子 。

2.

We want it in	white.
	2 days.

➡ 我們要白色的 。
我們兩天內就要 。

3.

The	catalogue item product	number is 90-0-2356.

➡ 目錄號碼 / 細目號碼 / 產品編號是九〇-〇-二三五六 。

4.

We will pay by	COD.
	credit card.
	money order.

➡ 貨到時我們會付款 。
我們會以信用卡 / 匯票付款 。

** COD 貨到收款（ *collect on delivery* ）　　*money order* 匯票

5.

| Could you | deliver it
bring it over
send it | by tomorrow? |

➡ 你能不能明天以前送到？

6.

Please make sure there are no defects in the
　merchandise.
Please handle the items carefully.
We won't accept any damaged goods.

➡ 請保證貨品完好無缺。
　請小心運送貨品。
　我們不會接受破損的貨品。

** defect〔dɪ'fɛkt〕n. 瑕疵

EXERCISE / 練習

◉ 模仿前面範例，完成下列對話。

　　Ikea：Ikea Furniture.
Secretary：This is Johnson Corporation. I would like
　　　　　　to _____ 2 _____ cabinets. We want
　　　　　　them in_____. The_____ number is
　　　　　　90-0-2356.

    Ikea: How _____ do you want it?

Secretary: Could you _____ by tomorrow afternoon?

KEY TO EXERCISE /解答 ░░░░░░░░░░░░░░░░░░

1. place an order for, office-style, white, product, soon, deliver it

2. order, office-style, black, item, quickly, bring it over

➤A TIP FOR YOU /秘書小點子

▶ 常用辦公用品的名稱 ◀

ball-point pen（原子筆）	calculator（計算機）
carbon paper（複寫紙）	cellophane tape（透明膠帶）
correction fluid（修正液）	desk calendar（桌曆）
envelope（信封）	eraser（橡皮擦）
folder（卷宗夾）	glue（膠水）
name card holder（名片薄）	paper clip（紙夾）
paper knife（裁紙刀）	pen（鋼筆）
rubber band（橡皮圈）	ruler（尺）
scissors（剪刀）	stapler（釘書機）
stationery（文具）	waste paper basket（廢紙簍）

附 錄

△商業英文書信(Business Letter)

寫信是秘書的例行工作之一，不論是公司往來的商業書信（ business letter ），或是上司私人的社交信函，都常由秘書代筆。一般而言，社交信函的書寫較為自由；而商業書信則屬**正式信函**，有固定格式，秘書必須特別注意。以下就商業英文書信的結構，作重點說明。

① **Letterhead** / 信頭文字

在信紙上端，印著公司的標誌圖案、公司名稱、地址、電話號碼、傳真號碼等。這種有信頭文字的信紙，只用於商業書信的**第一頁**。

② **Date** / 日期

日期打在信頭文字下幾行的位置。通常是按照月、日、年的順序來表示，如：*August 15, 19*××。日的後面須打上**逗點**，月通常不用縮寫。

③ **Inside Address** / 收信人姓名地址

在日期下幾行，由左端起，打上收信人姓名、公司名稱及其地址。

例：*Mr. Philip Crown, President* …… 收信人姓名、職稱
World Trading Co., Ltd. ……………… 公司名稱
90 Main Ave., Salt Lake City, ⎫
Utah 94839 USA ⎭ ………… 地址

收信人的姓名之後可加上他的**正式職稱**，通常先在姓名後打逗點，再接職稱。地址的寫法，從**門牌號碼**開始，依次是街名、區（或郡）名、都市（或縣）名、國名。在門牌號碼和街名間通常不加逗點。

④ **Salutation** / 開頭稱呼語

寫給公司行號的信，Salutation通常用 *Dear Madam(es),* *Dear Sir(s)* 或 *Gentlemen*。後面接冒號或逗點均可。

⑤ **Subject Line** / 主旨

信文中不一定要包含此項，但如果有 Subject Line，可使對方一看就知道本文的內容。一般是先打 *Re:* 或 *Subject:* 再接主旨。有時可加上底線，或全部用大寫。位置在 Salutation 下面空一行，由信紙中央或左端打起。

⑥ **Body** / 本文

是信文的主體，由 Salutation（或 Subject Line）下空二行寫起，每段開頭通常內縮幾個字（*Indented form*）。本文應以明確、簡潔爲尚。

① **DREXLER CORPORATION**

Exporters & Importers

7F #36 Fuhsing North Road, Taipei

Tel:(02)705-5413　Fax:(02)703-5572

② January 9, 19xx

③ Mr. Mark Lee, Import Manager
90 Main Ave.,
Salt Lake City, Utah
94839 USA

④ Dear Sir,

⑤ Subject: Product Inquiry

⑥　　　We are pleased to inform you that we do
sell the item which you have inquired about.
We've been in this business for a long time
and I'm sure you'll find our prices and qual-
ity very competitive. I'm enclosing a copy
of our price list and a catalogue of our products for your perusal. Should you have any
question please don't hesitate to contact us.

　　　Thank you for your inquiry and we hope
to be doing business with you soon.

⑦ Yours truly,

⑧ *Michael Baker*
Michael Baker
General Manager

⑨ MB/ss
⑩ Enclos. 1 Catalogue
　　　　　1 Price List
⑪ cc: Mr. James Smith

商業書信範例

⑦ **Complimentary Close** / 信尾客套語

常用的有 Sincerely, Sincerely yours, Yours sincerely, Truly yours, Yours truly 等，後面須接**逗點**。

⑧ **Signature** / 簽名

由 Complimentary Close 下面空二行開始，以大寫字母打出公司名稱（可省略），再由執筆者**親筆簽名**，最後打上執筆者**全名與職稱**。

⑨ **Identification Marks** / 識別記號

為表示負責，於信紙左下角打上執筆人（用大寫）與打字員（大、小寫均可）的姓名第一個字母，中間用斜線或冒號隔開。如：*SE / pr*，*TB : AL*

⑩ **Enclosure** / 附件說明

信內有一個附件時，要標明 *Enc.*，有二件以上時，則用 *Enclos.* 再打附件的名稱與件數。

⑪ **cc**（carbon copy）/ 副本收受人姓名

位置在 Enclosure 下方，打上信函副本收受人的姓名，以供收信人參考。

⑫ **Postscript**（P.S., PS）/ 附記

作補充說明之用，位置在信紙最下方，由左端寫起。商業書信應盡量避免使用 Postscript。

△ 會議紀錄 (Minutes of Meeting)

雖然各公司所採用的會議紀錄（ minutes of meeting ）不盡相同，基本上仍包含以下範例所列，秘書可做參考。

```
          Minutes of the Meeting of the
       CAREER DEVELOPMENT COMMITTEE
               June 18, 19xx

Presiding: Michael Baker

Present:      -------------
              -------------
              -------------

Absent:       -------------

The monthly meeting of the Career Development
Committee was called to order at 9 a.m. in
the Board Room by Michael Baker. The minutes
of the meeting of May 17 were read by......
and approved.

(The contents of discussions to be typed in
here. 紀錄會議內容。)

The meeting adjourned at 10 a.m.
```

||||||||||| ● **學習出版公司門市部** ● |||||||||||

台北地區：台北市許昌街 10 號 2 樓 TEL：(02) 3314060・3319209

台中地區：台中市綠川東街 32 號 8 樓 23 室
　　　　　TEL：(04) 2232838

||||||||||||||||||||||||||||||||||||||||||||||||||||||

秘書英語自學手冊

編　　著／陳　瑠　琍

發　行　所／學習出版有限公司　　　☎ (02) 7045525

郵　撥　帳　號／0512727-2 學習出版社帳戶

登　記　證／局版台業 2179 號

印　刷　所／裕強彩色印刷有限公司

台 北 門 市／台北市許昌街 10 號 2 F　　☎ (02) 3314060・3319209

台 中 門 市／台中市綠川東街 32 號 8 F 23 室　　☎ (04) 2232838

台灣總經銷／學英文化事業公司　　　　☎ (02) 2187307

美國總經銷／Evergreen Book Store　　☎ (818) 2813622

售價：新台幣一百五十元正
1997 年 3 月 1 日一版三刷

ISBN 957-519-020-3